Hayner Public Library District - Alton

0 00 30 0421883 4

No Longer the Property of
Hayner Public Library District

Warman's
COMPANION

ROSEVILLE
POTTERY

JUN 1 4 ···

BRANCH

HAYNER PUBLIC LIBRARY DISTRICT
ALTON, ILLINOIS

OVERDUES .10 PER DAY MAXIMUM FINE
COST OF BOOKS. LOST OR DAMAGED
BOOKS ADDITIONAL $5.00 SERVICE CHARGE.

Mark F. Moran

©2006 Krause Publications

Published by

krause publications
An Imprint of F+W Publications

700 East State Street • Iola, WI 54990-0001
715-445-2214 • 888-457-2873

Our toll-free number to place an order or obtain
a free catalog is (800) 258-0929.

All rights reserved. No portion of this publication may be reproduced
or transmitted in any form or by any means, electronic or mechanical,
including photocopy, recording, or any information storage and retrieval
system, without permission in writing from the publisher, except by a
reviewer who may quote brief passages in a critical article or review to
be printed in a magazine or newspaper, or electronically transmitted on
radio, television, or the Internet.

Library of Congress Catalog Number: 2005935067
ISBN 13-digit: 9-780896-893054
ISBN 10-digit: 0-89689-305-7

Designed by Marilyn McGrane
Edited by Dennis Thornton

Printed in China

Table of Contents

Introduction   4

Patterns

A Six-Decade Experiment

Collectors of Roseville Pottery become quite animated when discussing "experimental" pieces, those with trial glazes or unusual forms that never went into large-scale production.

In fact, the entire 64-year history of the company was one long experiment, first by trying to gauge public tastes, and finally by just trying to survive.

Ohio was the center of pottery production in the late 19th century, due to easily accessible waterways and an abundance of raw materials. Natural gas deposits in the Zanesville area, combined with rich clay, provided an ideal foundation for local potteries and gave Zanesville its nickname, "Clay City."

The Roseville Pottery Company, located in Roseville, Ohio, was incorporated on Jan. 4, 1892, with George F. Young as general manager. The company had been producing stoneware since 1890, when it purchased the J. B. Owens Pottery, also of Roseville. Wares included flowerpots and cuspidors, and all were unmarked. "Venetian" baking pans, "German Cooking and Farm Ware," the "Blended" line of jardinières and pedestals, and coin banks and novelties were some of Roseville's earliest products.

The popularity of Roseville Pottery's original lines of stoneware continued to grow. The company acquired new plants in 1892 and 1898, and production started to shift to Zanesville, just a few miles away. By about 1910, all of the work was centered in Zanesville, but the company name was unchanged.

Young hired Ross C. Purdy as artistic designer in 1900, and Purdy created Rozane—a contraction of the words "Roseville" and "Zanesville." Rozane was a style of brown underglaze pottery that was already popular at the time. Rozane was similar to artwares in production at two other Zanesville potteries: Weller Pottery's "Louwelsa" and the Owens Pottery's "Utopian." All of these Zanesville firms were imitating Cincinnati's Rookwood Pottery, which had developed its "Standard Glaze" line in 1884. The first Roseville artwork pieces were marked either Rozane or RPCO, both impressed or ink-stamped on the bottom.

In 1902, a line was developed called Azurean, which was similar to Weller's blue Louwelsa: a blue and white underglaze decorated artware on a blended background. Some pieces were marked Azurean, but often RPCO. In 1904 at the St. Louis Exposition, Roseville's Rozane Mongol, a high-gloss oxblood red line, captured first prize, gaining recognition for the firm and its creator, John Herold.

Other artists included Gazo Fujiyama—who created the Woodland, or Fujiyama, line as well as Rozane Fudji. Many Roseville lines were a response to the innovations of Weller Pottery, and in 1904 Frederick Rhead was hired away from Weller as artistic director. He created the Olympic and Della Robbia lines for Roseville. (He later designed the Fiesta wares for the Homer Laughlin Co.). His brother Harry took over as artistic director in 1908, and in 1915 he introduced the popular Donatello line.

By 1908, all handcrafting ended except for Rozane Royal. Roseville was the first pottery in Ohio to install a tunnel kiln, which increased its production capacity.

Frank Ferrell, who was a top decorator at the Weller Pottery by 1904, was Roseville's artistic director from 1917 until 1954. This Zanesville native created many of the most popular lines, including Pine Cone, which had scores of individual pieces.

Roseville patterns introduced under Ferrell's direction also include:

Futura (1928), Imperial II (1930 glazes), Earlam (1930), Ferella (1930), Sunflower (circa 1930), Montacello (1931),

Windsor (1931), Jonquil (circa 1931), Ivory (1932), Baneda (1932), Blackberry (circa 1932), Cherry Blossom (1933), Tourmaline (1933), Artcraft (1933), Falline (1933), Wisteria (1933), Laurel (1934), Topeo (1934), Luffa (1934), Russco (1934), Velmoss II (1935), Morning Glory (1935), Orian (1935), Clemana (1936), Primrose (1936), Moderne (1936), Moss (1936), Thorn Apple (1937), Dawn (1937), Ixia (1937), Poppy (1938), Teasel (1938), Fuchsia (1938), Iris (1939), Cosmos (1939), Crystal Green (circa 1939), Bleeding Heart (1940), White Rose (1940), Columbine (1941), Rozane Pattern (1941), and Bushberry (1941).

Many collectors believe Roseville's circa 1925 glazes were the best of any Zanesville pottery. George Krause, who had become Roseville's technical supervisor —responsible for glaze—in 1915, remained with Roseville until the 1950s.

Company sales declined after World War II, especially in the early 1950s when cheap Japanese imports began to replace American wares, and a simpler, more modern style made many of Roseville's elaborate floral designs seem old-fashioned.

In the late 1940s, Roseville began to issue lines with glossy glazes (Wincraft, Ming Tree, Artwood, and Lotus). Roseville tried to offset its flagging artware sales by launching a dinnerware line—Raymor—in 1953. Raymor was designed by Ben Siebel, but the style was rather austere when compared to better-selling dinnerware, and the line was a commercial failure.

Roseville issued its last new designs in 1953. On Nov. 29, 1954, the facilities of Roseville were sold to the Mosaic Tile Company.

Condition and Pricing

Since many of the Roseville pieces listed in this book were sold at auction, the descriptions are very detailed, down to the length of hairlines and the position of "flea-bite" nicks. Most price guides list values assuming a piece is in mint condition, but the prices here reflect the reality that very few examples of pottery survive for decades without at least minor wear or damage.

Reproductions

Since the mid-1990s, Roseville Pottery fakes and reproductions have been a growing problem. The best way to learn about reproductions is to visit The Roseville Exchange, whose motto is "dedicated to helping the public spot reproduction (fake) Roseville Pottery." You can find it online at http://www.ohi-oriverpottery.com/roseville_exchange/roseville.html. The site offers information on hundreds of reproductions—with style numbers and images—contributed by collectors, and side-by-side comparisons with real pieces.

Words of Thanks

This book would not have been possible without the generosity of:

David Rago Auctions, 333 N. Main St., Lambertville, NJ 08530. Phone: (609) 397-9374. Fax: (609) 397-9377. Web site: http://www.ragoarts.com/. E-mail: info@ragoarts.com.

The Iridescent House, 227 First Ave. SW, Rochester, MN 55902. Phone: (507) 288-0320. Web site: http://www.iridescenthouse.com.

Adamstown Antique Gallery, 2000 N. Reading Rd., Denver, PA 17517. Phone: (717) 335-3435. Web site: http://www.aagal.com/.

Antiques of Red Wing, 307 Main St., Red Wing, MN 55066. Phone: (651) 385-5963. E-mail: antiquesofrw@mcleodusa.net.

Memory Maker Antiques, 415 Main St., Red Wing, MN 55066. Phone: (651) 385-5914.

Apple Blossom

Introduced in 1948, this pattern features irregular leafy apple branches—some of which form handles—with clusters of white blossoms on blue, green, and pink backgrounds. The pieces have raised marks with style numbers.

Above: Apple Blossom blue wall pocket (366-8").
$200-$250
Left: Apple Blossom blue vase (393-18"), raised mark.
$1,200-$1,400

Apple Blossom blue tea set (371), raised marks; teapot: 7" by 11".
$550-$650

Apple Blossom blue basket (316-15"), raised mark.
$250-$300

Seven Apple Blossom blue pieces: pair of low candlesticks, hanging basket, center bowl, basket, dish, and vase, all marked.
$500-$600/set

Apple Blossom green basket (310-10"), raised mark.
$200-$250

Apple Blossom green jardinière (303-10") and pedestal (306-10"), jardinière has several chips at base and flakes to flowers, normal abrasion to top of pedestal, both marked.
$450-$550

Apple Blossom green jardinière (303-10"), glaze chip and bruise to base and some small glaze flakes to petals, raised mark.
$175-$225

Apple Blossom green vase with squat base (388-10"), raised mark.
$150-$200

Apple Blossom green pedestal (300-10"), raised mark.   **$110-$140**

Apple Blossom green wall pocket (366-8"), repair to handle (some paint flaking), raised mark.   **$110-$140**

Apple Blossom pink tea set (371), all marked.
$375-$425/set

Apple Blossom pink hanging basket, repair to rim chip and light abrasion to decoration, 5 1/2" by 8". **$90-$110**

Apple Blossom pink pillow vase (390-12"), flat chip to base, raised mark. **$125-$175**

Four Apple Blossom pink pieces: pair of planters (300-4"), rectangular planter (368-8"), and fan vase (373-7"), all marked. **$325-$375/set**

Apple Blossom pink vase (389-10"), raised ark, 10 1/8" by 4 3/4" by 6". **$350-$400**

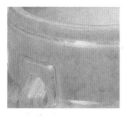

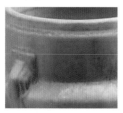

Artcraft

Introduced in 1933, Artcraft combined art deco influences and usually the earth tones of green and brownish tan, sometimes blue-green, occasionally with shades of pink and dull gold. The sleek, simple design features blunt buttressed supports and squat bases on the jardinières. The pieces are unmarked or have a foil label.

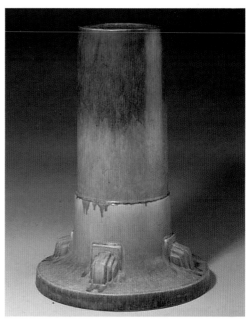

Above: Artcraft pedestal covered in shaded blue and green matte glazes, underglaze chip to base, and a few minute flecks to rim, unmarked, 17" by 9". **$900-$1,100**
Left: Artcraft brown pedestal, 3/4" chip to base, two small glaze flakes to top, and short tight line, unmarked, 17" by 11".   **$450-$500**

Artcraft jardinière in an oxblood glaze typical of the Topeo of Mowa lines, unmarked, 6 1/8" tall.
$700-$800

Artcraft jardinière with four buttresses, covered in a shaded green, rose, and yellow matte glaze, spider lines to base, chips to foot ring, and line from rim, 7" by 10". **$250-$300**

Artcraft jardinière in an Earlam glaze of mottled turquoise and lavender with a tan interior, unmarked, 4 1/8" tall.
$450-$550

Pair of small Artcraft jardinières with atypical black and white glazes, unmarked, white is 4 1/4" tall, black is 4" tall. **$500-$600 each**

Artcraft jardinière with four buttresses at the shoulder, exterior in light green and mottled blue, tan interior, 4 1/4" by 5 3/4". **$400-$450**

Two green Artcraft jardinières: silver foil label on one, 9 1/2" diameter and 5 1/2" diameter. **$750-$850/pair**

Artcraft brown planter, foil label, 5" by 7 1/4".
$200-$250

Artware and Landscape

Decorated Artware and Landscape pieces reflect the art nouveau influence at the turn of the 19th century. Designs included glossy, idealized landscapes with birds, and fruit and floral motifs.

The highly stylized motifs in the Landscape line were created both with squeeze-bag decoration and layers of clay (sgraffito) around the turn of the 19th century, and most were found on jardinières, pedestals, and umbrella stands. None are marked.

Left: Landscape jardinière and pedestal by Fredrick H. Rhead, decorated in squeeze-bag with flying geese over stylized fruit trees on the jardinière, and a landscape with stone wall on the pedestal. Jardinière has restoration to several chips and 5" V-shaped hairline from rim, overpainting around base (possibly from lifting overglaze), and several minor nicks to squeeze-bag; pedestal has restoration to 6" crack from top, and damage to overglaze on horizontal line halfway around neck; both pieces marked with artist's cipher; jardinière: 12 1/2" by 18", pedestal: 29" by 13 3/4". **$1,500-$1,700**

Decorated Artware jardiniere painted with red poppies on a shaded green, ochre and ivory ground, embossed with lion heads forming two handles; some flaking, nicks, and lines, unmarked, 12" by 16". **$150-$200**

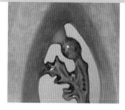

Artwood

Introduced in 1951, Artwood's most significant feature is the irregularly shaped opening in the sides of vessels—referred to by the company as "picture" elements—which are pierced by tree branches or flowers. The glossy mottled glazes include yellow, brown, green, blue, gray, and lavender. Pieces are marked "Roseville U.S.A."

Artwood green vase with pinecones (1060-12"), raised mark. **$250-$300**

Artwood Ikebana vase with thistle (1059-10"), covered in a glossy green and brown glaze, raised mark. **$400-$450**

Artwood Ikebana vase with cypress tree (1052-8"), covered in a glossy yellow and brown glaze, raised mark. **$250-$300**

Artwood yellow corseted vase with thistle (1059-10"), minor flake to inner rim, raised mark. **$80-$100**

Artwood Ikebana vase (1055-9") decorated with an oak branch, and covered in a glossy green and brown glaze, raised mark. **$450-$500**

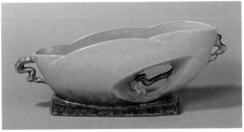

Artwood oval planter with cherry blossom branch (1062-12"), covered in a glossy brown and yellow glaze, raised mark. **$350-$400**

Artwood gray Ikebana flaring vase (1057-8"), decorated with a chestnut branch, raised mark. **$250-$300**

Artwood gray three-piece planter set consisting of an Ikebana vase (1051-6") decorated with nasturtium (minor flat nick under base) and two small side sections (1050), raised marks. **$300-$350/set**

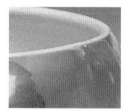

Autumn

Circa 1912, Autumn is a line of jardinières, planters, pitchers, basins, and chamber pots, all with transfer decoration of deciduous trees against a woodland landscape. The typical color combination is a blend of yellow with glossy red-orange or terra-cotta rims and bases, but other hues—including blues, greens and pinks—are known. Fewer than 20 shapes have been identified, and are usually unmarked.

Autumn jardinière (480-10"), unmarked.　**$350-$450**

Aztec

Introduced in 1904 and strongly influenced by the art nouveau movement, the name "Aztec" is a misnomer. This line featured stylized floral and geometric designs—with the occasional ship or Moorish arches—applied with slip cup or squeeze bag. Background colors include blue (from pale to navy), russet, gray, ivory, teal, and tan. Most are unmarked.

Aztec vase with bulbous shoulder and tapering body, decorated with stylized flowers and swags in white, yellow, and blue on a blue-gray ground, some burst bubbles and some minor nicks, unmarked, 11" by 4 1/2". **$350-$400**

Aztec blue trumpet-shaped vase decorated in polychrome squeeze bag with a garland pattern, light abrasion to some spots on white decoration, unmarked, 11" by 5". **$275-$325**

Aztec corseted vase with trillium squeeze-bag detail, glaze scaling to rim and base, one fleck to decoration, unmarked, 8 1/4" by 3 3/4". **$250-$300**

Right: Aztec blue pitcher, unmarked, 5 1/2" by 7". **$550-$650**

Azurean

Introduced shortly after the turn of the 19th century, this line featured hand-painted scenes or floral motifs done in varying shades of blue on a shaded white background. Many are signed by the artist and/or marked with an impressed "RPCo."

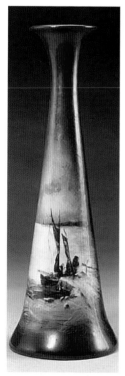

Left: Azurean vase decorated with fishing boats, 8" by 3". **$2,000-$2,100** Courtesy Adamstown Antique Gallery

Far Left: Azurean trumpet-shaped vase decorated by F.S. with fishermen in their boats, restoration to top, stamped "865/RPCo./2.," 18" by 6 1/2". **$1,400-$1,600**

Two Azurean vases, both painted with flowers, both with indistinct marks:
Right: two-handled, 8 1/4" tall. **$900-$1,000**
Left, ovoid, 6 3/8" tall. **$450-$550**

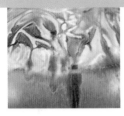

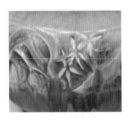

Baneda

Introduced in 1932, the name comes from the design motif which features a wide band that encloses spiky leaves, vines, and pods, often in dripping glazes of green, blue, orange, and yellow. Backgrounds are mainly green or pink, rarely blue. Pieces are unmarked or have a foil label.

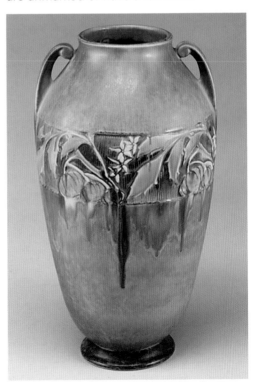

Baneda green bulbous vessel with collared rim and good mold and color, black paper label, 9 1/2" by 5". **$1,500-$1,700**

Baneda green bulbous vase with very strong mold and color; two flat chips to foot ring (do not show on side), unmarked, 15 3/4" by 7 3/4". **$3,200-$3,300**

Baneda green jardinière with crisp mold and good color, unmarked, 8" by 11 1/2". **$2,400-$2,600**

Baneda green flaring vase with good mold, glaze pimple to rim, unmarked, 12 1/4" by 7 1/4". **$1,100-$1,300**

Baneda green bulbous urn, bruise and restored chip to rim, crisp mold, good color, unmarked, 10" by 9". **$800-$900**

Baneda green bulbous urn with strong mold, unmarked, 6 1/4" by 4". **$600-$700**

Baneda green spherical vase, unmarked, 5 1/2" by 6 1/2". **$700-$800**

Baneda green bulbous urn, bruise and restored chip to rim, crisp mold, good color, unmarked, 10" by 9". **$800-$900**

Baneda green milk-can shaped vase, very tight bruise and opposing short hairlines to rim, unmarked, 7 1/4" by 5 3/4". **$350-$400**

Baneda pink urn with crisp mold and color, unmarked, 12 1/4" by 9 3/4".
$1,300-$1,500

Baneda pink planter, small, with good mold, pock mark, unmarked, 4 1/4" by 5 1/2". **$275-$325**

Baneda pink bulbous urn with very strong mold and color, silver foil label, 9 1/4" by 7 3/4".
$850-$950

Baneda pink candlesticks, unmarked, 5 1/2" by 3 1/2". **$450-$500/pair**

Baneda pink bulbous urn with strong mold and color, 1/2" crazing line to rim, foil label, 7" by 7".
$400-$500

Baneda pink faceted bowl with 1" bruise to one handle, silver foil label, 3 1/4" by 11". **$350-$400**

Baneda pink pear-shaped vase, minor bruise to one handle, unmarked, 5 1/2" by 4 1/2". **$250-$300**

Baneda pink bulbous vessel, foil label, 4 1/4" by 4 1/2". **$250-$300**

Baneda pink milk-can shaped vase with strong mold, unmarked, 7" tall. **$450-$550**

Baneda pink flaring wall pocket, restoration to chip at rim, and short, tight firing line to back, unmarked, 8 1/4" by 7 1/2". **$1,900-$2,100**

Baneda pink flaring vase with strong mold, unmarked, 7 1/4" by 4 1/4". **$550-$650**

Baneda pink ovoid vase, silver foil label, 6 1/4" by 3 1/2". **$350-$450**

Banks

Because they were usually given to youngsters, these banks rarely survived without some damage, and many were broken to get at the money inside. Dating from the early 1900s, shapes included cats, dogs, pigs, birds, and even a buffalo and Uncle Sam. They were simply and crudely glazed in mottled brown, yellow, green, and red, and were unmarked.

Left: Two early banks: one of an eagle's head marked "Souvenir/Sheboygan, Wis." on a mottled yellow and green ground, and one buffalo in mottled beige, unmarked, 2 3/4" by 3 1/2" and 3 1/4" by 6". **$400-$500/pair**

Three early banks: one of Uncle Sam, one monkey on a chamber pot, and one jug inscribed "Ye Olden Time" (minor fleck to rim), in assorted glazes, unmarked; 4 3/4" by 3 1/2", 5 3/4" by 3", and 4 1/4" by 3 1/2". **$350-$400/set**

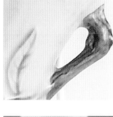

Bittersweet

Like the invasive deciduous perennial, Bittersweet pieces are wrapped in leafy green vines with reddish-yellow flowers and woody handles. Introduced in 1951, backgrounds are gray, green, and yellow; the mark is usually raised.

Left: Bittersweet footed vase (863-4"), 6" by 4 1/8" by 5 3/8". **$150-$200**

Two Bittersweet vases (885-10"), one gray and one yellow, both marked. **$300-$350/pair**

Three Bittersweet vessels: green double planter (858), yellow pillow vase (884-8"), and yellow planter (841-5"), all marked.   **$275-$325/set**

Bittersweet yellow wall pocket (866-7"), small flake to foot, raised mark.
$150-$200

Left: Bittersweet wall pocket, unmarked, 7" by 4 5/8" by 2 1/2".   **$400-$500**

Bittersweet gray vase (885-10"), raised mark.
$125-$175

Four Bittersweet pieces: gray basket (808-6"), yellow vase (885-10"), green basket (810-10") with chips and cracked handle, and small bowl (826-6"), all marked.
$275-$325/set

Blackberry

Introduced about 1932, this line features a collar of russet and green leaves, dark blue berries, and a textured background in varying shades of brown and green. The pieces are unmarked or have foil or paper labels.

Blackberry bulbous urn with collared rim, strong mold, minute fleck to rim, two stilt-pull chips, unmarked, 12 1/4" by 8 1/4". **$900-$1,000**

Blackberry basket, very small nick to one berry, unmarked, rare, 7 1/2" by 6". **$1,000-$1,100**

Blackberry flaring wall pocket, unmarked, 7 3/4" tall. **$1,200-$1,400**

Blackberry two-handled vase with crisp mold and good color, unmarked, 6 1/4" by 5 1/2". **$500-$600**

Blackberry bulbous vessel, strong mold and color, black paper label, 5 1/4" by 4 1/2". **$400-$500**

Blackberry bulbous vase (#575) with good mold, unmarked, 8 1/4" by 5 1/4". **$600-$700**

Pair of candlesticks with good mold and color, gold foil label to one, 4 1/2" by 4". **$500-$600**

Blackberry bulbous vase, 4" line from rim, unmarked, 6 1/4" by 5 1/2". **$300-$350**

Blackberry bulbous two-handled vase, touch-up to fleck on one handle, unmarked, 5" by 4 3/4". **$225-$275**

Blackberry spherical planter with two short rim handles, 1/2" chip to inner part of one handle, small bruise to rim, unmarked, 6 1/4" by 7 1/2". **$350-$400**

Blackberry faceted planter, unmarked, 3 1/2" by 9 3/4". **$300-$375**

Left: Blackberry shouldered vessel, unmarked, 6 1/4" by 5 1/2". **$400-$500**

Blackberry squat vessel, unmarked, 4 1/2" by 6". **$300-$350**

Blackberry low bowl, strong color, minor glaze bubbles, minute pinprick to rim, unmarked, 3 1/4" by 7 3/4". **$250-$300**

Two Blackberry bulbous vases: the larger with restored inner rim chip, the smaller with burst bubbles throughout, unmarked, 6 1/4" tall and 5 1/4" tall. **$375-$425/pair**

Roseville POTTERY **27**

Bleeding Heart

Introduced in 1940, the pink flowers and pale or mottled green leaves stretch across backgrounds that include blue, green, and pink. This pattern has a raised mark: "Roseville U.S.A."

Bleeding Heart blue tapering vase (976-15"), 1/2" bruise to bottom, raised mark. **$650-$750**

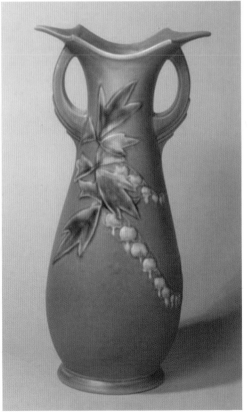

Bleeding Heart pink floor vase (977-18"), restoration to two points on rim, small chips to inner base ring (do not show on side), raised mark, rare.
$325-$375

Bleeding Heart blue basket (360-10"), raised mark. **$350-$400**

Left: Two Bleeding Heart blue pieces: flaring vase (964-6") and small jardinière (651-3"), crisp molds, raised marks.
$600-$700/pair

Below: Three Bleeding Heart blue pieces: bowl (382-10") and a pair of flaring vases (962-5"), all marked. **$350-$400/set**

Bleeding Heart blue corseted vase with squat base (969-8"), raised mark. **$750-$850**

Two Bleeding Heart blue pieces: faceted vase (968-8") and cornucopia (141-6"), raised marks.
$850-$950/pair

Two Bleeding Heart ewers, one blue (972-10") with crisp mold, and one green (963-6"), raised marks.
$650-$750/pair

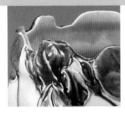

Blended

Though sometimes called majolica, that name does not really capture the frequent linear and swirling themes of the Blended line, introduced in the early 1900s. The colors, however, are similar to majolica hues, and were applied to jardinières, pedestals, and sand and umbrella holders. Pieces are often unmarked or occasionally have incised marks.

Blended jardinière and pedestal (414), each with embossed lion's head handles and covered in a brown, green, and yellow flambé majolica glaze, some hairlines and several chips to both pieces, unmarked; jardinière: 12 3/4" by 20", pedestal: 21" by 13".   **$500-$600**

Blended umbrella stand impressed with stylized arches under a brown, yellow, and forest green majolica glaze, a few shallow scratches and minor pockmarks to decoration, incised mark "727," 20 1/4" by 9 1/4".
$375-$425

Blended Iris jardinière, as-is condition (lines, bruises, chips), unmarked, 11" by 12". **$300-$350**

Blended jardinière (422) in streaked maroon and charcoal glazes, unmarked, 11 1/2" tall. **$350-$400**

Blended jardinière (458) with a motif of swimming fish in a green glaze, unmarked, 8" tall. **$250-$300**

Blended jardinière (479) in dripping rose, yellow, and green glazes with a raised design of stylized flowers and vines, unmarked, 8" tall. **$250-$300**

Pair of Blended jardinières, left, (406) in raspberry and turquoise, 6 5/8" tall, $125 to $150; right, (407) in cobalt and chartreuse, 5 3/4" tall. **$100-$125**

Burmese

Featuring stoic-faced male and female heads in green, black, or ivory, the Burmese line from 1950 included bookends, sconces, and candleholders. Pieces usually have raised marks.

Left: Two Burmese green sconces (80-B), raised marks, 8" tall.
$200-$225/pair

Right: Two Burmese green wall plaques (72-B and 82-B), raised marks, 8" tall.
$350-$375/pair

Left: Pair of Burmese black sconces (80-B), raised marks, 8" tall.
$175-$200/pair

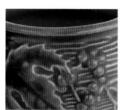

Bushberry

Introduced in 1941, Bushberry has large three-section leaves with sawtooth edges and clusters of berries. The handles are stylized branch forms, and the textured background colors are blue, brown (really more of a terra cotta red), and green. Pieces feature raised marks.

Bushberry green planter (778-14"), flat chip and bruise to base, raised mark. **$900-$1,100**

Bushberry green floor vase (41-18"), some small flat chips to base, light glaze scaling, and minor bruise to one berry, raised mark. **$350-$450**

Bushberry blue basket (371-10"), raised mark.
$275-$325

Bushberry blue three-piece tea set: teapot (2-T), creamer (2-C), and sugar dish (2-S), chips to sugar dish and creamer, and minute fleck to berry on teapot, raised marks; teapot: 6" by 10 1/2".
$225-$275

Bushberry blue basket (370-8"), with crisp mold, raised mark. **$175-$225**

Three Bushberry blue pieces: cylindrical vase with twisted handles (32-7"), with restoration to very minor flat chip at base, and two cups (1- 3 1/2"), one with line from rim, all marked.
$175-$225/set

Bushberry green vase (37-10"), strong mold and color, small chip to one berry, raised mark.
$225-$275

Five Bushberry vases: three blue and two green (28-4", 156-6", 30-6", 657-3"); restoration to rim of one, and bruise to base of another, all marked.
$400-$450/set

Bushberry brown handled vase (31-7"), 7 3/4" by 5 3/8" by 4 1/2".
$225-$275

Three Bushberry pieces: brown bud vase (152-7") with nicks at base and a pair of blue vases (35-9"), with nick to berry and repair to chip at base of one, raised marks. **$250-$300/set**

Bushberry brown small planter (657-3"), raised mark, 4 5/8" by 3".
$125-$150

Four Bushberry brown pieces: basket (370-8") with crack to handle, small planter (657-3") with repaired base and fleck to handle, flat vase (36-9") with fleck to leaf, and bowl (416-12") with three flecks to rim, all marked.
$300-$350/set

Bushberry brown basket (372-12"), large repair to chips at base, two re-glued cracks to handle, two small chips to handle, raised mark, unusual form. **$110-$140**

Cameo I and II

Another line with art nouveau influence, the Cameo motif (circa 1910) featured two distinct themes: females in profile in a woodland setting, and a classical Greek scene with horsemen, all on jardinières and pedestals. The piece seen here is identified as Cameo II. Both Cameo I and II are unmarked.

Below: Cameo II jardinière with cherubs and columns, in green, brown, and ivory glazes, unmarked, 9" tall. **$400-$500**

Right: Cameo II vase with cherubs and columns, in green brown and ivory glazes, bruise to one nose, unmarked, 8" by 4 1/4" **$175-$225**

Three Cameo II vases with cherubs and columns, in green, brown, and ivory glazes, all unmarked, left: 8" tall; center, 9 7/8" tall; right, 7 7/8" tall. **$300-$400 each**

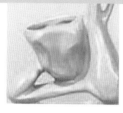

Capri

From 1950, Capri was made in vivid glossy or mottled colors in shapes that were borrowed both from nature and from the period taste for sleek and sinuous forms. Pieces have raised marks.

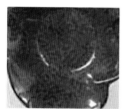

Six Capri pieces: four dishes (527-7") and two planters (558), in assorted glazes, all marked; planters: 7" by 6".
$200-$250/set

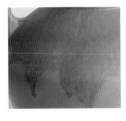

Carnelian I and II

Carnelian I and II are distinctly different in both shape and color. Carnelian I, circa 1910, has dripping glazes in shapes based on classical vessels. Colors include gray, dull green, blue, and a yellow that's more of an ochre. Ink stamps are common, but some are unmarked.

Carnelian II, circa 1915, are generally heavier and simpler in appearance and the mottled, dripping glazes include amber, green, purple, red, pink, teal, and mauve. Pieces are unmarked or have a paper label.

Carnelian I yellow post-factory lamp base with fittings, several small chips and lines, unmarked; pottery: 15 1/2" tall. **$275-$325**

Unusual Carnelian I-shape bulbous vase covered in an experimental turquoise, gray, and brown dripping glaze, "Rv" ink stamp, 7" tall. **$400-$500**

Carnelian I tall ewer in gray and buff, restoration to spout, "Rv" ink stamp, 15 1/4" tall. **$225-$275**

Carnelian I green ovoid vase with restoration to chip at base, "Rv" ink stamp, 10 1/4" tall.
$90-$110

Carnelian I handled vase, tan over pale green glaze (319-9"), bottom ink stamp "R," 9 1/2" by 9".
$450-$525

Two Carnelian I yellow bulbous vases, "Rv" ink stamp to both, 8" and 7".
$275-$325/pair

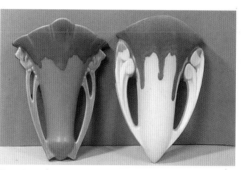

Carnelian I spherical vase covered in a dripping green glaze over a pale pink ground, restoration to chip at rim, "Rv" ink stamp, 8 1/4" by 10 1/2".
$125-$175

Two Carnelian I wall pockets: one covered in a dripping gray over pink glaze, and one in two shades of green; "Rv" ink stamps, 8 1/2" tall each.   **$300-$400/pair**

Two Carnelian I yellow pieces: a flat vase and a bulbous vase (chip to base), "Rv" ink stamp to both, 6" and 7 1/2" tall.   **$90-$110/pair**

Carnelian I vase with buttressed supports, dark green dripping glaze on pale green body, unmarked, 6" by 5 1/8" by 4".
$150-$175

Carnelian II ewer covered in a mottled pink glaze with purple drips from rim, repairs to handle, remnant of paper label, 15" tall. **$550-$650**

Carnelian II spherical vase covered in a fine frothy green, purple, and pink glaze, glaze losses inside foot ring, unmarked, 8 1/2" by 8 1/2". **$1,400-$1,600**

Carnelian II faceted center bowl covered in a fine green, purple, and amber glaze, a few nicks to base, unmarked, 4" by 15". **$225-$275**

Carnelian II red bulbous vase, some grinding chips, unmarked, 7" by 4 1/2". **$350-$400**

Right: Carnelian II vase with squat base and buttressed flaring neck, covered in a frothy pink and green glaze, a few very minor flakes to base, unmarked, 16 1/2" by 11 1/4". **$2,800-$3,200**

Carnelian II squat two-handled vase, a few short tight lines to rim, repair to chip under one handle, unmarked, 6 1/2" by 9". **$150-$200**

Carnelian II urn covered in a frothy teal and mauve glaze, unmarked, 10" by 6 1/2". **$250-$300**

Carnelian II ovoid vase with slightly flaring rim, covered in mottled mauve, green, and ochre glaze, some burst bubbles, unmarked, 7 1/2" tall. **$225-$275**

Carnelian II classically shaped vase covered in mottled mauve, brown, and ochre glaze, unmarked, 9" by 5 1/4". **$350-$400**

Carnelian II urn in green and pink frothy matte glaze, unmarked, 9 1/2" by 10". **$400-$450**

Carnelian II vessel covered in a deep green to rose glaze, minute nick to base, unmarked, 3 1/2" by 6". **$250-$300**

Carnelian II wall pocket in a frothy pink and ochre glaze, black paper label and gift shop tag, 7 1/2" by 5 3/4". **$325-$375**

Early Carnelian lamp base, unmarked, 12" by 6 1/4". **$300-$400**

Early Carnelian planter or window box, unmarked, 8 3/4" by 3" by 3 1/2". **$150-$200**

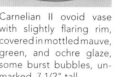

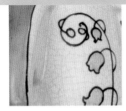

Ceramic Design

Ceramic Design was a wide-ranging collection of styles and decoration, early 20th century, that borrowed freely from other Roseville lines in both shape and glaze, especially for urns, wall pockets, and planters. Most pieces are unmarked.

Ceramic Design wall pocket (331), unmarked, 10 3/4". **$650-$750**

Ceramic Design wall pocket (330), unmarked, 11 3/4" long. **$650-$750**

Ceramic Design wall pocket with restoration to tip, unmarked, 10" tall.
$250-$300

Ceramic Design wall pocket (328), 10 3/4" long.
$500-$600

Ceramic Design creamware sugar bowl and creamer, enamel-decorated with forget-me-nots, hairline and chip to sugar bowl handle, unmarked, 3" and 4 1/2" tall.
$60-$80/pair

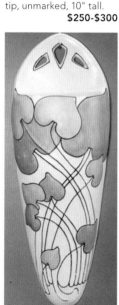

Ceramic Design wall pocket with five very small flat chips to back, and restoration to larger chip, unmarked, 18" tall.
$1,100-$1,300

Ceramic Design planter with spade-shaped flower and checkered design, covered in a matte green glaze, several repairs to feet, unmarked, 10 1/2" by 12 1/2". **$450-$550**

Cherry Blossom

Introduced in 1933, Cherry Blossom features a radiating pattern of contrasting stripes and textured ground overlaid with blossoming cherry branches. The brown and beige background is more common than the pink and green. Most pieces are unmarked or have a paper or foil label.

Cherry Blossom brown ovoid vase, unmarked, 12" by 6 3/4". **$800-$900**

Cherry Blossom pink two-handled vase, unmarked, 10 1/2" by 6 1/2".   **$1,300-$1,400**

Cherry Blossom brown squat vessel, foil label, 4 1/4" by 5 1/2". **$200-$250**

Cherry Blossom brown planter, unmarked, 4" by 5". **$200-$250**

Cherry Blossom brown bulbous vase, unmarked, 5" by 6 1/2". **$300-$350**

Cherry Blossom pink jardinière with small clay pimples around flower and one short crazing line to rim, gold foil label, 4" by 5 1/2". **$350-$400**

Cherry Blossom brown spherical vase, minor nick to one blossom, unmarked, 8 1/2" by 7 1/4". **$600-$700**

Cherry Blossom brown spherical vase with crisp mold, foil label, 8" by 7 3/4". **$650-$750**

Cherry Blossom brown vase with squat base, foil label, 8 1/4" by 5". **$450-$500**

Cherry Blossom brown ovoid vase, flea-bite to rim, unmarked, 10 1/4" by 6 1/4". **$600-$700**

Cherry Blossom brown wall pocket, unmarked, 8" tall. **$950-$1,050**

Chloron

Using many of the molds also found in Egypto and Matt Green, Chloron (circa 1908) is a dull green with raised motifs of flowers, leaves, figures, and faces. Some pieces have contrasting ivory panels. Pieces are often unmarked, but occasionally occur with an ink stamp.

Chloron wall sconce with owl on ivory panel (339), 12 1/2" by 12 1/2".
$2,500-$3,000

Chloron wall pocket with face framed in grape clusters and leaves (346), 9 5/8" by 9".
$1,800-$2,200

Chloron tapering two-handled vessel with scalloped rim, the body embossed with cherries, stamped "Chloron/T.R.P. Co.," 6 1/2" by 7". **$1,200-$1,300**

Chloron vase with raised grapes and leaf design, shape C22, stamped "Chloron/ T.R.P. Co.," 8 1/4" tall. **$400-$450**

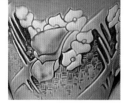

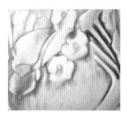

Clemana

Sources vary on the introduction year of Clemana, ranging from 1934 to 1936. The design features stylized white flowers and green leaves on a striated pattern similar to long narrow thorns. Background colors are blue, brown, and green. Pieces have an impressed mark.

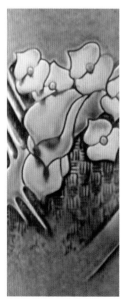

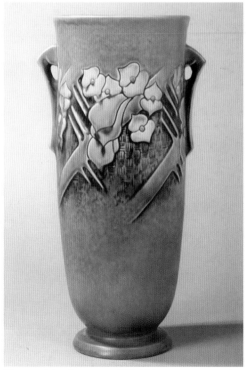

Clemana blue flaring urn (759-14"), restoration to chip on one handle and rim and several around base, impressed mark.   **$550-$650**

Two Clemana brown bulbous vases: 751-7" with restoration to chips at rim and base, and 752-7", impressed marks.
$275-$300/pair

Two Clemana blue vases: (752-7") and (749-6") with minute stilt-pull, impressed mark. **$450-$500/pair**

Clemana green flaring vessel (753-8"), minor fleck to rim, impressed mark. **$275-$300**

Clemana blue chalice (122-7"), impressed mark. **$350-$400**

Two Clemana green vases: 752-7" with restoration to chips at rim and base, and 750-6", impressed marks. **$300-$350/pair**

Left: Two Clemana brown vessels: one bulbous (754-8") with two chips to bottom, and one footed (122-7"), impressed marks. **$375-$400/pair**

Clemana green spherical vase (754-8"), restoration to one handle, impressed mark. **$175-$225**

Clematis

Introduced in 1944, Clematis features broad blossoms of six or seven petals and a trailing ivy vine (that bears little or no resemblance to real clematis leaves) on a textured background of blue, brown, or green. Pieces have raised marks.

Clematis green cookie jar (3-8"), raised mark, 9" by 10 1/4". **$800-$900**

Clematis green bulbous vase (107-8"), raised mark, 8 1/4" by 6 3/4" by 6 1/2".
$175-$200

Clematis green bud vase (192-5"), 5 1/8" by 6" by 3 5/8". **$150-$200**

Clematis green fan/cornu-copia vase (193-6"), raised mark, 6 1/4" by 6 1/4" by 3 5/8". **$125-$150**

Clematis green tea set (5) with some pockmarks to base and several small chips under foot ring of teapot, burst bubble to spout, and minor glaze miss to base of creamer, raised marks; teapot: 7 3/4" by 11".
$200-$250/set

Three Clematis green pieces: small basket (387-7") with repair to large portion of handle and base, larger bas-ket (389-10") with fleck and bruise to base, and urn (188-6"), raised marks. **$175-$225/set**

Clematis blue wall pocket, unmarked, 8 1/8" by 5 3/4" by 2 5/8". **$325-$375**

Clematis blue low handled bowl (459-10"), 13 3/4" by 11 1/2" by 4". **$300-$350**

Clematis blue tea set, comprised of a teapot (5), creamer (5-C) with small chip at base, and sugar bowl (5-S) in as-is condition (chips and cracks), raised marks. **$125-$175**

Three Clematis pieces: blue basket (387-7") with filled-in chip to base, blue fan vase (193-6"), and green bulbous vase (188-6"), all marked. **$150-$200/set**

Far left: Clematis blue cookie jar (3-8"), two large chips to base, flecks inside lid, and chip to one flower, raised mark. **$110-$140**

Left: Two Clematis blue cornucopia vases (141-8"): drilled hole to base of one and three chips to base of the other, raised marks. **$35-$50/pair**

Five Clematis brown pieces: double bud vase (194-5") with nick and small repair, bud vase (187-7") with repaired rim, bulbous vase (102-6"), another bulbous vase (103-6") with repaired handle, and triple vase (192-5") with small chip to base, all marked. **$175-$225/set**

Clematis brown cookie jar (3-8"), bruise and small nicks to lid, and bruises and nicks to jar, marked. **$200-$250**

Three Clematis brown pieces: triple bud vase/flower frog (50) with spider cracks, rectangular planter (391-8") with nick to handle, and console bowl (458-10") with reglued chips, all marked. **$110-$140/set**

Clematis brown ewer vase (16-6"), 6" by 6 1/2" by 6 1/4". **$175-$225**

Left: Two Clematis brown pieces: bulbous vase (107-8") and ewer (17-10"), raised marks. **$175-$225/pair**

Clematis brown bulbous vase (103-6"), raised mark, 6 1/4" by 5" by 4 1/2". **$150-$200**

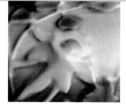

Columbine

Introduced in 1941, Columbine has a large bloom on tall slender stems with trailing leaves and three-leaf clusters. Background colors are blue, brown to green, and pink to green. Pieces have raised marks.

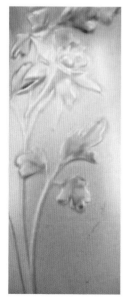

Columbine blue tall bulbous vase (27-16"), raised mark.
$425-$475

Columbine blue basket (368-12"), raised mark.
$350-$450

Columbine blue hanging basket, 2" bruise to rim, burst bubble to one hole, unmarked, 4 3/4" by 8".
$110-$140

Pair of Columbine blue bookend planters (8), raised marks, 5 1/4" by 5" by 5". **$200-$250/pair**

Three Columbine blue pieces: squat vase (399-4") and a pair of candlesticks (1145-2 1/2"), all marked.
$150-$200/set

Three Columbine ewers (18-7"): one pink with a few small chips under foot ring, one brown, and one blue, raised marks.
$325-$375/set

Four Columbine pieces: brown urn (151-8") and three bulbous vases (12-4"), two brown and one pink (chip to rim), all marked. **$275-$325/set**

Columbine brown basket (365-7"), raised mark.
$225-$275

Columbine brown classically shaped vase (23-10"), good mold and color, raised mark.
$200-$250

Pair of Columbine brown planter bookends (8), raised marks, 5 1/4" by 5" by 5". **$200-$250/pair**

Columbine squat vessel (655-3"), 3" by 5 1/4".
$200-$250

Two Columbine vases: one brown (150-6") with crisp mold and 1/4" glaze bubble to flower, and one blue (22-9"), raised marks. **$225-$275/pair**

Columbine pink vase (21-9"), raised mark, 9 1/4" by 6 3/8" by 5 3/4".
$225-$275

Columbine pink vase (24-10"), raised mark, 10 3/8" by 7 3/4" by 6".
$200-$250

Columbine pink basket (367-10"), pinhead size fleck on one stem, raised mark. **$175-$225**

Three Columbine pieces: two planters, one blue (655-3") and one pink (399-4"), and a pink vase (16-7"), chips to each, one reglued, all marked. **$150-$200/set**

Columbine pink candlesticks (1145-2 1/2"), both marked. **$90-$110**

Corinthian

A successor to Donatello, Corinthian (circa 1923) features a radiating fluted design in green and ivory with a band of entwined grape vines and fruit below a modified egg-and-dart border. Pieces are unmarked or with an "Rv" ink stamp.

Corinthian wall pocket, "Rv" ink stamp, 9 1/4" tall. **$200-$225**

Corinthian wall pocket, "Rv" ink mark, 9 1/2" tall. **$250-$300**

Corinthian hanging basket with small nick to hanging holes, unmarked, 8 3/4" wide. **$150-$200**

Cosmos

Introduced in 1939, Cosmos features clusters of large blossoms on a contrasting irregular band, set against a textured background of blue, brown, or green. There is a mix of raised and impressed marks, or foil labels.

Cosmos green basket (358-12") with restoration to crack at rim, raised mark. **$110-$140**

Cosmos green footed basket planter (358-12"), soft mold, raised mark. **$400-$450**

Cosmos green handled vase with buttressed base, unmarked, 18 1/2" by 8 1/2" by 9 1/4". **$1,000-$1,200**

Two Cosmos green pieces: flaring vase (947-6") and squat vessel (375-4") with several small nicks to decoration and base, raised marks. **$175-$225/pair**

Cosmos blue two-handled vase (948-7"), impressed mark.
$175-$225

Cosmos blue spherical basket (357-10") with two chips to petals and chip to handle, raised mark.
$175-$225

Cosmos blue floor vase with scalloped, flaring rim (958-18"), very good mold and color, minute fleck to rim, possibly in firing, raised mark. **$650-$750**

Two Cosmos blue pieces: double bud vase (133-4 1/2") with some grinding chips to base, and rectangular planter (381-9") with good mold, raised marks.
$300-$350/pair

Cosmos blue double wall pocket (1266-6"), silver foil label. **$500-$600**

Three Cosmos bulbous planters: green and brown (649-3"), and blue (649-4"), raised marks.
$250-$300/set

Cosmos blue flowerpot
with under plate (650-5"),
soft mold, raised mark.
$175-$225

Two Cosmos footed urns
(135-8"): one blue (with
foil label) and one brown,
one has restoration to
cracked foot and fleck to
petal, raised marks.
$200-$250/pair

Cosmos brown footed
basket planter (357-10"),
raised mark. **$200-$250**

Two Cosmos ewers (957-15"): one brown with some minor flakes to high points and one green with reglued
spout and flakes to high points, impressed marks.
$400-$450/pair

Cosmos brown ewer (955-
10"), impressed mark.
$300-$350

Cosmos brown urn (956-
12"), restoration to rim
chip, raised mark.
$225-$275

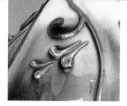

Cremo

The Cremo line is among the rarest Roseville patterns, and consequently among the most expensive. The undulating forms introduced about 1912 have tiny stylized flowers and stems draped on glossy glazed vessels with colors that blend from dusty pink at the top to yellow, streaked green, and dark green. They are unmarked.

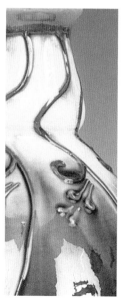

Cremo vase, shape No. 11, 7 3/4" tall.   **$1,400-$1,500**

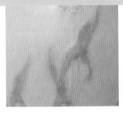

Cremona

Introduced in 1927, Cremona featured a diffuse or mottled pastel background of celadon green (sometimes fading to pale yellow or gray accents) or dusty pink (pale blue is rare), with stylized flowers and leaves in various simple arrangements. Pieces are unmarked or have foil labels.

Cremona green bulbous vase with two handles, unmarked, 10 1/4" by 6". **$250-$300**

Cremona green vase with buttressed handles near rim, decorated with small roses and leaves, unmarked, 8 1/4" by 3 3/4". **$225-$275**

Cremona green baluster vase, unmarked, 12 1/4" tall. **$325-$375**

Left: Cremona green pillow vase, minor nick to rim and dark crazing line to foot, unmarked, 6" by 6 1/2". **$45-$55**

Cremona pink flaring vase with two buttressed handles at rim, unmarked, 12" by 6". **$250-$300**

Cremona pink vase with lavendera freesia, burst bubbles to rim, unmarked, 12 1/4" by 4". **$175-$225**

Cremona pink shouldered vase with flaring rim, unmarked, 10" by 6". **$175-$225**

Cremona flaring vase in pink and green glazes, unmarked, 8" by 5 1/2". **$150-$175**

Cremona pink four-sided vase with blue blossoms, small chips at base (show very slightly on side) and 1" chip to rim, unmarked, 10" by 4". **$150-$200**

Cremona pink low bowl and flower frog, the bowl with pumpkins around its edges, unmarked, 2 3/4" by 8 1/2" diameter; frog, 1 1/2" by 3 3/4" diameter. **$225-$275**

Creamwares

The Roseville creamwares, most of which date from 1910 to 1920, included the Juvenile line, novelty steins, fraternal items, smoker sets, shaving mugs, and even pin boxes. They were rarely marked.

Three Creamware mugs, decorated with an Indian, and the emblems of the Fraternal Order of the Elks and Eagles, between 4 1/2" and 5" tall. **$200-$250/each**

"Good Night" candleholder, unmarked, 6 1/2" by 4 1/2" by 6" (with handle, not shown). **$500-$600**

Eight assorted transfer-printed pieces: "F.O.E." tankard and two mugs; two "Should Auld Acquaintance..." mugs; Quaker Children small dish; Kosair commemorative mug, 1934; and Knights of Pythias pipe stand; some minor chips, heights range from 12" to 2 1/2". **$350-$400/set**

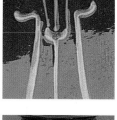

Crocus

Introduced about 1912, Crocus features stylized flowers and line decoration regularly spaced around the vessels using the squeeze-bag technique. Pieces are unmarked or have artist initials.

Crocus bulbous vase with stepped rim, squeeze-bag decorated in blue, yellow, and green, unmarked, 6" tall. **$850-$950**

Courtesy Adamstown Antique Gallery

Crocus

Crocus green jardinière with four buttressed handles, touched-up 2 1/2" bruise to rim, scratches, and several pock marks, unmarked, 9" by 12". **$650-$750**

Crocus bulbous vase, restoration to glaze chips at base, fleck to rim, 9 3/4" by 4". **$300-$350**

Left: Two Crocus vases, both with stylized floral motifs, right: bottle vase, unmarked, 6 7/8" tall, **$450-$550**; left, three-sided vase, unmarked, 8 1/8" tall. **$650-$750**

Two Crocus vases and an Aztec oil lamp, all with stylized floral motifs, right: cylindrical, unmarked, 9 3/4" tall, **$600-$700**; oil lamp, unmarked, 11" tall, **$750-$850**; left, bottle form, unmarked, 9 1/4" tall. **$550-$650**

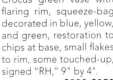

Crocus green vase with flaring rim, squeeze-bag decorated in blue, yellow, and green, restoration to chips at base, small flakes to rim, some touched-up, signed "RH," 9" by 4". **$300-$350**

Crystalis

Introduced about 1905 and part of the Rozane Wares, Crystalis is usually found in a speckled gold and ivory glaze, and pieces often have arching or angular buttressed supports. Pieces are unmarked or have a paper Rozane Ware label.

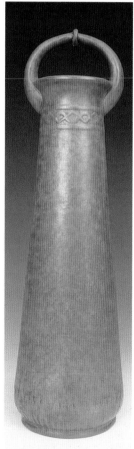

Above: Crystalis squat vessel with buttressed supports around neck, 4" by 6 1/4". **$1,800-$1,900**
Right: Crystalis ring-handle vase in an Egypto shape (E 58) with a mottled salmon and gold glaze, some restoration, with "Rozane Ware/Egypto" wafer, 14 7/8" tall. **$1,500-$1,800**
Courtesy Adamstown Antique Gallery

Dahlrose

Dating from the 1920s, Dahlrose features large daisy-like blossoms with brown centers on a textured body that changes from muddy green to terra cotta brown. Pieces are unmarked or have paper labels.

Dahlrose bulbous vase with strong mold, unmarked, 10" by 9". **$1,000-$1,200**

Dahlrose jardinière and pedestal, several small chips and lines, un-marked; jardinière: 8 1/4" tall; pedestal: 16 1/2" tall. **$450-$500**

Dahlrose rectangular planter, good mold, unmarked, rare in this size, 6 1/4" by 13". **$500-$600**

Dahlrose bulbous vessel with flaring rim, excellent mold and color, black paper label, 9 1/4" by 7".
$800-$900

Dahlrose footed urn with flaring rim, black paper label, 12 1/4" by 9".
$450-$550

Dahlrose bulbous vase, some glaze inconsistency to flowers, unmarked, 10" tall.
$200-$250

Dahlrose jardinière, 1/2" chip to base, unmarked, 8" by 11".
$225-$275

Dahlrose rectangular planter, some minor nicks, excellent condition overall, unmarked, 6 1/4" by 12".
$300-$350

Dahlrose flower pot with under plate, short firing line to rim of pot and short tight line to rim of under plate, unmarked, 5 1/2" by 6".
$200-$250

Dahlrose shouldered vessel with two short handles, shallow firing line to body, unmarked, 6 1/4" by 8".
$150-$175

Dahlrose bulbous vase, touch-up to base, small bruise to one handle, unmarked, 8" by 7".
$125-$175

Two Dahlrose vases: one tapering four-sided with good mold and minor chip inside foot ring, and bud vase with buttressed handles, unmarked, 6 1/4" by 3 1/2" and 8 1/4" by 5". **$450-$550/pair**

Two Dahlrose pieces: bud vase and bulbous planter, black paper labels, 8 1/4" tall and 4 1/2" by 6 3/4". **$350-$400/pair**

Two Dahlrose pieces: four-sided vase with flaring rim (restored chips at rim) and flat vase with strong mold (some small chips at base and tight line to rim), unmarked, 6" and 6 1/4" tall. **$325-$375/pair**

Dahlrose wall pocket, chip to tip, 10 1/4" tall. **$125-$175**

Left: Two Dahlrose pieces: squat vessel and an oval planter, latter has soft mold and minute fleck to one handle, unmarked, 4 1/2" by 6 1/2" and 4 1/2" by 10 1/2". **$225-$275/pair**

Two Dahlrose pieces: triple bud vase with strong mold and bulbous vase, black paper label to one, 6 1/4" and 8 1/2" tall. **$275-$325/pair**

Dahlrose console set consisting of a small oval center bowl and a pair of candlesticks, minute fleck to handle of one candlestick, unmarked; bowl: 10 1/2" diameter; candlesticks: 3 1/2" tall. **$250-$350/set**

Two Dahlrose pieces: small jardinière (two minor repaired chips to base) and a planter (tight cracks and repaired rim), both unmarked; taller: 4 1/4". **$125-$175/pair**

Two Dahlrose pieces: urn with buttressed handles (crack to one handle, overpainted small chips at rim) and bulbous vase, unmarked, 10" by 7 1/4" and 6 1/4" by 4 1/4". **$275-$325/pair**

Dahlrose double bud vase, unmarked, 7 1/2" by 6 1/4" by 2 1/4". **$275-$325**

Dawn

Introduced in 1937, the art deco-influenced Dawn has a stark, spidery leaf decoration on soft green, pink, or yellow backgrounds, and most pieces have footed or buttressed bases. Examples have an impressed mark or foil label.

Dawn green cylindrical vase, restoration to rim chip, illegible mark, 11 1/4" by 7 1/2". **$400-$450**

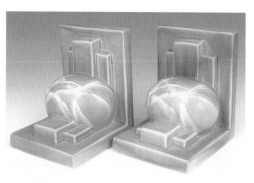

Pair of Dawn green bookends (4), impressed mark, 5 1/4" by 4 1/4" by 4 1/2". **$450-$500/pair**

Dawn yellow flower frog (31-3x4"), impressed mark. **$150-$175**

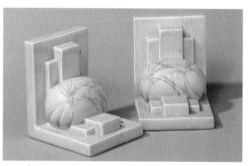

Pair of Dawn pink bookends (4), impressed mark, 5 1/4" by 4 1/4" by 4 1/2" **$450-$550/pair**

Dawn green spherical jardinière (316-6"), minor fleck to corner of one handle, another to corner of base, foil label and impressed mark.
$250-$300

Left: Two Dawn pink vases (826-6" and 829-8"), impressed marks.
$300-$350/pair

Dealer's Signs

Easily damaged, dealer's signs command a premium in mint condition. Most date from the second quarter of the 20th century and come in a range of glaze colors. New signs are being made, so beware of reproductions.

Dealer's sign in blue, 4" by 9 3/8".
ww **$2,800-$3,000**

Dealer's sign in green, 4 1/4" by 9 1/2".
$2,600-$2,800

Dealer's sign, 4 5/8" by 7 1/2".
$2,500-$2,800

Dealer's sign in blue and yellow glazes, glaze miss to top of "L," 5" by 8".
$2,100-$2,300

Dealer's sign in pink, 2 1/4" by 6 1/4".
$1,200-$1,400

Dealer's sign with light pink letters on a deep rose matte ground, restoration to several chips, 6 1/4" long. **$800-$900**

Left: Dealer's sign, 1 1/2" by 5 1/2".
$1,400-$1,500

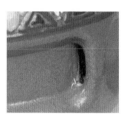

Decorated Matt

The line called Decorated Matt evolved from other Roseville patterns popular between 1905 and 1910, and reflects influences of the art nouveau and arts & crafts movements. Soft colors of dusty blue and tan for backgrounds are contrasted with bold geometric and stylized forms from nature in cream, yellow, navy, and terra cotta. These pieces are usually unmarked, but may include an artist's signature.

Decorated Matt jardinière in gray-blue with geometric design along rim in cream, yellow, and brown, unmarked, 6 1/4" tall. **$1,500-$1,800**

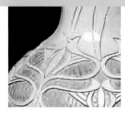

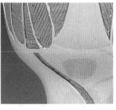

Della Robbia

Designed by Frederick H. Rhead about 1905 as part of the Rozane Wares, and named for a 15th century Florentine family of sculptors and ceramists famous for their enameled terracotta or faience, the Della Robbia group is the most complex and diverse collection of Roseville pieces, as well as the rarest. Borrowing freely from centuries of decorative themes—stretching from ancient Greece to the American Arts & Crafts movement—Della Robbia is the Holy Grail of Roseville collectors. A Della Robbia vase holds the world auction record for a piece of Roseville, selling for $38,850 in 1999.

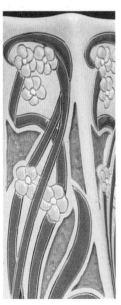

Della Robbia spherical vase, shape No. 10, with five bands of daisies, Rozane Ware wafer, 8" tall.
$2,800-$3,000

Della Robbia vase, twisted four-sided form with tiny lavender blossoms and sinuous dark green leaves, marked twice with an inscribed "E," 9 3/4" tall. **$2,500-$2,800**

Della Robbia oil lamp, shape D-6, in sage and cream with large stylized leaves and blossoms, Rozane Ware wafer, 11 1/8" tall. **$2,000-$2,200**

Della Robbia vase, cylindrical with stylized flowers on a brown background, 10" by 5", wafer mark and incised artist initials. **$5,000-$6,000**

Della Robbia teapot excised with hearts, cups and saucers, and Japanese fans, in brown and celadon, small nicks to lid, 1" clay burst to rim of pot and 1/2" chip to base, Rozane Ware wafer, 9" by 8" **$1,100-$1,200**

Della Robbia pillow vase, shape No. 5, with a large stylized blossom in sage and dark green, Rozane Ware wafer, 7 3/8" tall. **$2,200-$2,400**

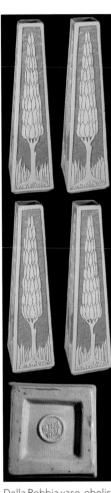

Della Robbia vase, unusual example with deeply carved and cut-back floral design, whiplash stems and leaves in a multitoned green glaze, signed with wafer mark, artist signed, 14" tall, two minor flakes. **$5,000-$6,000**

Della Robbia vase, obelisk form with stylized trees set on a tan background, wafer mark, 10 1/2" by 2 3/4". **$4,500-$5,000**

Della Robbia teapot, its lid with the inscription "Polly put the kettle on/ we'll all have tea/Sukie take it off again/it's all boiled away"; the body with two excised panels, each depicting a woman in a kitchen holding a kettle, in beige and brown, restoration to lid, several nicks and cracks to base, restoration to spout, Rozane Ware wafer, 5 3/4" by 7 1/2". **$500-$600**

Dogwood I and II

There are two distinct Dogwood patterns: textured (called Dogwood I, circa 1916) and smooth (called Dogwood II, mid-1920s). The earlier version has subtler shades and an olive-colored background; pieces were unmarked or ink stamped. The later pattern is a more intense green shot with brown, and the branches are nearly all black; pieces were seldom marked.

Dogwood I bulbous urn with good mold, crack to one handle, small pockmark to rim, "Rv" ink stamp, 12" by 7 1/2". **$800-$1,000**

Dogwood II almond-shaped planter, complete with original liner, good mold and glazing, 1" bruise to rim of planter, minor bruise to base, and several chips to liner, illegible stamp mark, rare, 6" by 11 1/4".
$900-$1,100

Dogwood II jardinière, restoration to rim chip and several glaze chips (some restored) to petals, unmarked, 8 1/2" by 10".
$175-$200

Dogwood I rectangular planter, complete with original liner, strong mold, good glazing, minor fleck to body, unmarked, 6 1/4" by 11 1/2".
$150-$175

Left: Two Dogwood I vessels: one squat (good mold, small glaze flake to petal) and one bulbous (several small flakes to petals), both have "Rv" ink stamps, 4" by 7" and 8 1/4" by 6 1/2".
$150-$200/pair

Two wall pockets: Dogwood I and double Dogwood II (small flake to tip), first one has "Rv" ink stamp, the other is unmarked, 9" by 5" and 8 1/4" by 6 1/2".
$400-$500/pair

Donatella

With a strong art nouveau influence, Donatella (circa 1912) was also part of the creamwares and featured geometric, cameo, figural, and floral motifs. These pieces are unmarked. The angular handles and long, narrow spots are easily damaged, so beware of restorations.

Donatella coffeepot and creamer (style E) decorated with a stylized floral motif; teapot 6 1/2" tall.

$600-$700/pair

Donatello

Also designed by Frederick Rhead, Donatello (circa 1915) had lighter green and beige fluting than Corinthian. A frieze of cherubs encircled the vessels with a brown background. Pieces were usually unmarked, or had an "Rv" ink stamp or paper label.

Donatello trial glaze jardinière and pedestal set with band of winged cherubs in the forest, lines to interior and one to base of jardinière, glaze flake to base of pedestal, unmarked, jardinière: 10" tall; pedestal: 18" tall.   **$650-$750**

Donatello bud vase (116-6"), 6 1/8" by 2 3/8".
$180-$220

Donatello vase, normal abrasion and small bruise to base, unmarked, 9 1/2" by 5 1/2". **$80-$100**

Donatello footed vase, unmarked, 10" by 4 1/2". **$110-$140**

Donatello jardinière and pedestal, chip repair inside rim of jardinière, "Rv" ink stamp to pedestal; pedestal: 18" by 11 1/2"; jardinière: 9" by 11". **$180-$220**

Pair of Donatello flaring vases, both with some nicks to rim, unmarked, 8" by 3 3/4" each. **$150-$200/pair**

Donatello bulbous vase, several flat chips to base, unmarked, 10 1/4" tall. **$300-$350**

Two Donatello pieces: pitcher (several flecks) and an unusual chamberstick (1/4" chip to base), unmarked; pitcher: 6 1/4" tall. **$125-$175/pair**

Two Donatello pieces: small basket and a wall pocket; bruise, line, and some nicks to rim of basket, chip go rear side of hanging hole; Donatello stamp mark to one, "Rv" ink stamp to other; 8" and 10 1/2" tall. **$175-$225/pair**

Donatello "gate" or double bud vase, black paper label, 7 3/4" by 4 3/8" by 2". **$125-$150**

Donatello cuspidor or spittoon, unmarked, significant crazing to interior, 7 1/2" by 5 3/8". **$225-$250**

Pair of Donatello baskets with arched handles, soft mold, one has short underglaze line to rim (does not go through) and minute fleck to one rib, unmarked, 9 1/4" by 6 1/4" each. **$450-$500/pair**

Dutch

Part of the creamware line, circa 1915, the Dutch transfer decoration was found on cups, pitchers, teapots, and other utilitarian wares. Pieces were unmarked.

Assorted Dutch mugs with transfer decorations, each between 4" and 5" tall, unmarked. **$80-$120 each, depending on condition.**

Tall Dutch pitcher (lemonade?), with transfer decoration, 11" tall, unmarked. **$250-$350**

Earlam

Introduced in 1930, Earlam combines soft glaze colors that blurred from tan to pink and blue to gray, with pale greens and light browns. The shapes are deceptively simple, echoing Chinese Neolithic pottery. Pieces are unmarked or have paper/foil labels.

Earlam green strawberry jar, unmarked, 8" by 6 1/2".
$800-$900

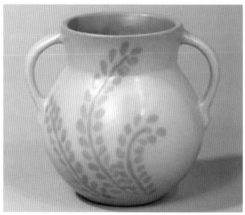

Earlam vase, shape 517, with trial glaze semigloss decoration of hand-painted leaves on a peach ground, marked "trial no. 38" under the base, 5 1/2". **$1,100**

Earlam ginger jar, V-shaped bruise to the inner part of the lid, gold foil label, 10 3/4" by 6". **$250-$300**

Earlam wall pocket, unmarked, 6 1/2" tall. **$750-$850**

Earlam brown two-handled vessel with four-sided rim, unmarked, 6 1/4" by 7 1/2". **$400-$450**

Earlam blue strawberry jar or planter, unmarked, 8" by 6 1/2". **$800-$900**

Earlam green four-sided planter with arched rim, unmarked, 5 1/4" by 10 1/4" by 2 1/2". **$225-$275**

Earlam two-handled vase with four-sided rim, in pink and blue, unmarked, 6" by 8". **$350-$400**

Pair of Earlam green chambersticks, black paper labels, 4" by 7". **$400-$500**

Early Wares

These pieces, usually pitchers and cuspidors, date from before 1920 and were part of the utility line. The raised and hand-painted images have a naïve folk art appeal and include animals, flowers, figures, and landscapes. None are marked.

Early pitcher with farm landscape, repair, and line to spout, unmarked, 7 1/2" by 8 3/4". **$60-$80**

Early pitcher known as "The Boy" (two views), un-marked, 7 1/2" tall, seen in as-found condition, if per-fect. **$400-$500**

Early pitcher with Dutch figures (called "No. 2 Hol-land"), 9 1/4" tall. **$200-$250**

Two early pitchers, one Iris and one with Dutchman (lines at rim possibly from firing, several glaze bursts), unmarked, 8 1/2" and 9" tall. **$175-$225/pair**

Early cuspidor with tulips in an indigo glossy glaze with gilded details, 1/4" chip to rim, abrasion to base, unmarked, 5 1/2" by 8". **$40-$60**

Two early pitchers with landscapes in as-is condition (chips, cracks, lines, touch-ups), unmarked, 7 1/2" tall each. **$125-$175/pair**

Two early pitchers, one with cow (a few short lines), the other with tulip (small chip to spout, hairline near handle), unmarked, 7 1/2" tall each. **$250-$300/pair**

Early pitcher in blended glaze, unmarked, 7 1/2" tall. **$200-$250**

Early pitchers: floral, unmarked, 9 1/2" tall, **$250-$300**; cow, unmarked, 7 1/2" tall. **$200-$250**

Early mug with a Dutch boy on one side and a Dutch girl on the other, 4" tall. **$60-$80/set of four**

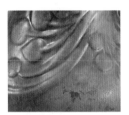

Egypto

Part of the Rozane Wares, Egypto (circa 1905) has less to do with Egypt and more to do with the American Arts & Crafts movement, with its soft green glaze and naturalistic forms. Sometimes unmarked, many pieces have a "Rozane Ware/Egypto" stamp on an applied wafer.

Egypto factory lamp base embossed with three Indian men on elephants, three factory drill holes, complete with a converted oil font, small chip and some unevenness to base, marked with Rozane Ware/Egypto wafer; 10 1/4" by 9" without font. **$2,800-$3,200**

Egypto vase embossed with lotus leaves and blossoms, all covered in a smooth vellum medium-green matte glaze, Egypto wafer, 8 1/2" by 8". **$3,700-$3,800**

Egypto tall tapering vase, its neck embossed with a band of diamonds, covered in a frothy matte green glaze, Rozane wafer, 12 1/2" by 4 1/4". **$1,700-$1,900**

Egypto inkwell and cover, fine and rare, of classical design, with Caesar medallion on lid, a wreath of laurels, columns, and classical motifs around drum base, all covered in a fine curdled matte green glaze, very tight line to rim, probably from firing, excellent overall condition, Egypto wafer, 3 3/4" by 5". **$600-$700**

Egypto corseted tankard, typical glaze pulling at base with minor grinding chips, unmarked, 10 1/2" by 5". **$750-$850**

Egypto squat two-handled vessel embossed with cherries and leaves, Egypto wafer, 5 1/2" by 7 1/2". **$600-$700**

Egypto oil lamp on tall tapering foot, embossed with lotus plants, hairlines to base, Egypto wafer, 9 1/2" by 9". **$650-$750**

Egypto pitcher in oil lamp form, unmarked, 5" by 6". **$550-$650**

Egypto urn embossed with pattern around neck, 1/2" chip to handle, Egypto wafer, 8 1/2" by 6 1/4". **$375-$425**

Egypto pitcher embossed with waves under a feathered matte green glaze, unmarked, 7 1/2" tall. **$500-$600**

Egypto vessel with scalloped rim and embossed broad leaves to body, unmarked, 5 1/4" by 5". **$400-$450**

Egypto bulbous two-handled vessel, fleck at base, burst bubbles throughout, unmarked, 5 1/2" by 5 1/4". **$300-$350**

Egypto bud vase, grinding chips, 5 1/2" by 2 1/2". **$450-$500**

Egypto urn with bulbous body and flaring neck, covered in a fine rich green semi-matte glaze, chip to rim and large stilt-pull chip to base, Rozane wafer, 9 3/4" by 4 1/2". **$275-$325**

Elsie

The Elsie juvenile ware set of bowl, cup, and plate was made in the late 1940s.

Borden Milk Company three-piece child's breakfast set commemorating Elsie the Cow and Beauregard the Bull, consisting of a plate (7 1/2" diameter), bowl (5 1/2" diameter) and mug (2 1/2" diameter), all covered in a glossy pumpkin glaze, minor wear to surface decoration on plate and bowl, raised marks.   **$750-$850**

Experimentals, Trial Glazes

Experimental pieces sometimes have incised names, style, and glaze numbers marked on the back or bottom.

Lady Slipper hand-carved experimental vase with yellow and white flowers on one side and a single flower with reverse coloration on the back, pink shading to sky blue, three sets of trial numbers for glaze, 8". tall.

$4,000

Experimental vase with painted Baneda-type design on a mottled brown and orange ground, possibly hand-thrown, touched-up fleck to one handle, unmarked, 4 1/2" by 7". **$1,000-$1,200**

Experimental urn decorated with band of blossoms, covered in a deep amber glaze with dark green interior, stilt-pull to base, numbered marks, 7" by 7 1/2". **$3,250**

Left: Experimental rectangular planter in the style of Thorn Apple, unmarked, 4" by 10". **$225-$275**

Experimental vase in the Arrowhead pattern, white blossoms and green leaves on a textured and smooth background of dusty blue, inscribed on reverse, "Arrowhead … Flowers-white … Leaves-green … Flower centres orange … Buds yellow green white edges," with glaze numbers written on bottom, 8 7/8" tall. **$3,000-$3,500**

Experimental vase in Mountain Laurel pattern, with white blossoms, green leaves and pink buds on a striated band of dull green set on a tan background, with glaze number written on bottom, 9 1/8" tall.

$3,000-$3,500

Lady Slipper experimental vase, with yellow and lavender flowers on a textured and smooth background of dusty green and tan, with glaze numbers on bottom and gold foil label, 8 1/4" tall.

$2,800-$3,200

Experimental vase with lavender geranium and leaves on a textured green and tan background, inscribed on reverse "Geranium" and marked on bottom with glaze numbers, 9 1/4" by 8 1/4".

$2,500-$2,800

Experimental gourd-shaped vase with two angular handles, decorated with laurel leaves in blue-green over a mottled raspberry glaze, marked with glaze codes on bottom, 5 1/2" by 5 1/4".

$2,100

Trial glaze plate with series of numbers representing color codes, 8" diameter. **$1,800**

Trial glaze two-handled bulbous vase covered in a shaded blue, green, and ochre matte glaze, shallow 1 1/2" scratch to body, unmarked, 9 1/4" by 8 1/4".

$500-$600

Left: Carved experimental urn on a high-glaze Tuscany blank, with impressed floral pattern in orange and green on a butter yellow ground, marked with glaze codes on bottom, 8 1/4" by 7". **$1,800**

Falline

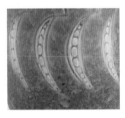

Still one of the most popular designs, Falline (early 1930s) is ringed by heavy sinuous forms separated in the middle by a pea-pod pattern that can be green, bluish, or yellow. Body colors include various shades of mottled pinkish-tan darkening to brown, and yellow-green blending with blue. Pieces are unmarked or have foil labels.

Falline blue bulbous vase with collared rim and curved handles, glaze inconsistency to one side, good mold and color, unmarked, 6 1/4" by 6 1/4". **$850-$950**

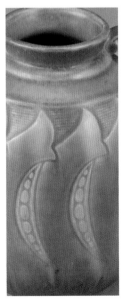

Falline brown bulbous vase with crisp mold, 1/2" chip to base, unmarked, 15 1/4" by 7 1/4".
$1,100-$1,300

Falline brown two-handled vessel with squat base, stabilized 4" Y-shaped lines from rim, restored shallow chip at base, remnant of foil label, 12 1/2" by 7".
$1,200-$1,400

Falline brown two-handled vase, unmarked, 8 1/2" by 6". **$450-$550**

Falline brown bulbous handled vase (644-6"), 6 3/8" by 6 1/4" by 5 3/4".
$900-$1,000

Falline brown bulbous two-handled vase, unmarked, 6 1/2" by 6 3/4".
$500-$600

Falline brown bulbous two-handled vase, foil label, 6 1/2" by 6 1/2".
$550-$650

Left: Falline blue low bowl, touch-up to handle and to rim, unmarked, 9 1/4" diameter.
$150-$200

Roseville POTTERY **99**

Falline blue ovoid two-handled vase, unmarked, 7 1/4" by 5 1/2"

$1,000-$1,200

Falline brown bulbous two-handled vase, unmarked, 6 1/4" by 4 3/4" by 3 3/8". **$950-$1,100**

Falline blue two-handled vase, Y-shaped crack through body, foil label, 6 3/4" by 5". **$325-$375**

Falline brown bulbous two-handled vase, unmarked, 7 1/2" tall.
$525-$575

Pair of Falline brown urns, crack from rim and 1/2" chip to base of one, 1/4" chip to base of other, remnant of store labels, 8 1/2" by 7". **$550-$650/pair**

Right: Falline blue bulbous two-handled vase, two minor bruises and a small repaired chip, all to one handle, unmarked, 7 1/2" tall. **$750-$850**

Far right: Falline brown flaring urn, unmarked, 6 1/4" tall. **$350-$450**

Ferella

Named for designer Frank Ferrell, the Ferella line (1931) features pierced borders and footed bases, both decorated with tiny stylized floral motifs that at first appear to be a shell pattern. Exterior colors include mottled brown and tan with pink or lavender hues, and raspberry red combined with green. Pieces are unmarked or have paper labels.

Green factory lamp base in the style of Ferella, restoration to top, remnant of foil label, 10 1/2" tall.
$800-$900

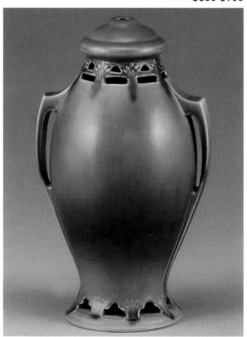

F

Ferella red beehive-shaped vessel, unmarked, 5 3/4" by 6 3/4".
$800-$900

Ferella red bud vase, unmarked, 6" by 4 1/2".
$600-$700

Ferella red flaring vase, unmarked, 5 1/4" by 4 1/4".
$500-$600

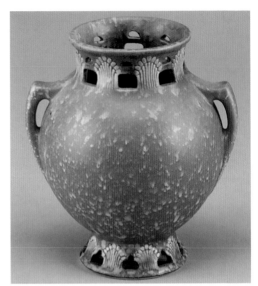

Ferella red bulbous urn, short tight line to rim, black paper label, 8" by 7 1/2".
$750-$850

Two Ferella red pieces: footed oval bowl with restoration to two long lines from rim, and squat vessel, unmarked; 5 1/2" by 12 3/4", and 4" by 6 1/2".
$650-$750/pair

Ferella brown bud vase, unmarked, 6" by 4 1/2". **$300-$400**

Ferella brown oval centerpiece bowl, 1" line from rim to cutout, unmarked, 5 1/2" by 13". **$650-$750**

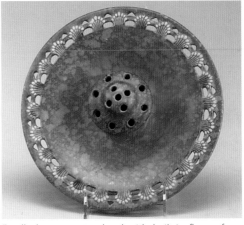

Ferella brown center bowl with built-in flower frog, black paper label, 9 1/2" diameter. **$525-$625**

Ferella brown footed ovoid vase, unmarked, 10 1/4" by 6". **$850-$950**

Right: Ferella brown vessel with flaring rim, remnant of black paper label, 5" by 6 3/4". **$550-$650**

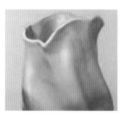

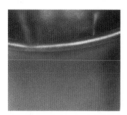

Florane I and II

There is some lingering debate as to the correct term for these two patterns. Some prefer to include Florane I with Rosecraft; others call Florane II "Etruscan." Three decades and a world of style difference separate the two. Florane I (circa 1920) did borrow from the classical Rosecraft shapes, but has more colors. Florane II (1949) has several billowing, twisted profiles and brighter hues. The former has ink stamps, the latter has raised marks.

Two Florane I baskets, both with "Rv" ink stamp, right: Rosecraft shape 310/9, 9 7/8" tall; left: Rosecraft shape 319/8, 8 3/8". **$350-$450 each**

Two Florane I pieces: vase (Rosecraft shape 244/6), "Rv" ink stamp, 6" tall, $200 to $250; low bowl (124/6) with separate flower frog (15/3 1/2); bowl 2 1/8" tall, 7 1/4" diameter, bowl marked with "Rv" stamp, frog unmarked. **$250-$300/pair**

Florane I flaring ovoid vase, "Rv" ink stamp, in a style also found in Lustre and Rosecraft-Color, 9" by 8". **$110-$140**

Five Florane II pieces: blue planter (64-12"), two green vases (81-7" and 80-6"), green planter (60-6"), and tan rectangular dish (407-6"), all marked. **$225-$275/set**

Florane I brown wall pocket, touch-up to tip, "Rv" ink stamp, in a style also found in Rosecraft-Color, 9 1/2". **$90-$110**

Left: Five Florane II planters (94-8", 90-4", 72-5" and 73-6"), four in matte blue and one in glossy beige, all marked. **$100-$125/set**

Florentine

Florentine had two incarnations, first in 1924 and again in 1940, sometimes called Florentine I and II. The earlier version comes in brown and ivory, and has rough textured brown panels regularly spaced and separated by garlands of grape vines and flowers, with a modified egg-and-dart rim. Pieces are unmarked or have an "Rv" ink stamp. The later version has textured brown and ivory panels separated by ivory partitions with green-glazed decoration and a green-trimmed rim. These pieces are unmarked or have a raised "Roseville U.S.A." mark.

Left: Florentine brown jardinière and pedestal, several minor hairlines, touch-ups to decoration, and restoration to both handles on jardinière; glaze inconsistencies around base of pedestal; jardinière: 10 1/2" tall; pedestal: 18 1/2" tall.   **$900-$1,200**
Right: Five Florentine brown pieces: bulbous vase (a couple minute flecks), corseted vase (small chip and a line), another bulbous vase, and two candlesticks (reglued base and bruise to rim of one), "Rv" ink stamp to four; tallest: 8 1/2". **$250-$300/set**

Florentine ivory umbrella stand, minor glaze burst near base and short tight spider line to underside of base (does not go through), unmarked, 20 1/2" by 10". **$275-$325**

Four Florentine brown vases: 8 1/2" vase in as-is condition; several small chips and bruises to the others, all marked; heights: 10 1/2", 8 1/2", 7 1/2", and 6 1/2".
$225-$275/set

Florentine brown jardinière with chip to one handle, unmarked, 8" by 11". **$250-$350**

Two Florentine pieces: ivory footed dish (some minor bruises and nicks to rim, a few small chips to body) and brown jardinière (bruise to one flower, chip and line to base), one marked, 4" by 10" and 7" by 9 1/2".
$90-$110/pair

Florentine brown hanging basket, "Rv" ink stamp, 4" by 7". **$125-$150**

Left: Florentine brown "gate" double candle-holder, unmarked, 9" by 4 1/2" by 2 3/4".
$120-$140

F

Foxglove

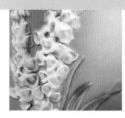

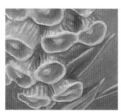

Foxglove

One of the most naturalistic patterns, Foxglove (1942) features tall, tapering blossom clusters of dusty white, pink, and yellow with green leaves on backgrounds of blue, green, and pink-brown. Pieces usually feature raised marks that say "Roseville U.S.A."

Foxglove green vase (55-16"), several flat chips to flowers and base (some possibly in making), raised mark.
$325-$375

Foxglove blue wall pocket (1292-8") with strong mold and color, minor nick to one flower, raised mark. **$350-$375**

Foxglove blue hanging basket with two pointed handles, stamped "U.S.A.," 5 1/2" by 10".
$175-$200

Four Foxglove green pieces: 43-6", 44-6" (repair under rim), 161-6" (bruise to handle), and 42-4", all marked.
$275-$325/set

Foxglove blue bulbous vase (418-4") with chip to each handle and crack to one, raised mark.
$60-$70

Two Foxglove pieces: a blue shell-shaped planter (426-6") with nicks to one end, and a green urn (162-8") with line to one flower, both marked.
$250-$300/pair

Pair of Foxglove green cornucopia vases (164-8"), reglued tip to one, raised marks. **$125-$175**

Two Foxglove green pieces: shell-shaped vessel with line and chips to rim, and vase (48-8"), raised marks.
$110-$140

Foxglove pink basket (373-8"), minute nick to one flower, raised mark. **$150-$200**

Two Foxglove pink pieces: console bowl (425-14") with chip and fleck to tip and a cornucopia vase (163-6") with minor peppering, raised marks. **$200-$250/pair**

Foxglove pink wall pocket (1292-8"), raised mark. **$225-$275**

Two Foxglove pink vases: 166-6" and 161-6", raised marks. **$200-$250/pair**

Right: Foxglove pink jardinière (418-6"), raised mark, 6 1/2" by 8 3/4" by 8 1/4". **$225-$250**

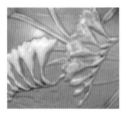

Freesia

Introduced in 1945, Freesia features rather stylized blossoms in fanning clusters of white, lavender, and yellow wrapped around the body of the vessels. Backgrounds are blended blues, brown-orange-russet, and greens. Most are marked—often raised, sometimes impressed.

Freesia blue tea set (6), raised marks; teapot: 7 1/2" by 11". **$350-$400/set**

Three Freesia blue pieces: tall ewer (21-15") with minor bruise near spout, flaring vase (124-9") with 1/4" chip to rim, and smaller vase (119-7"), all marked. **$400-$450/set**

Freesia blue cookie jar (4-8"), 1/2 inch bruise to rim and lid, a few small glaze nicks to high points (some from firing), raised mark. **$400-$450**

Two Freesia pieces: blue flaring vase (125-10") with restored chips to rim and green console bowl (466-10") with light scaling to rim, raised marks. **$90-$110/pair**

Freesia blue creamer (6C) and sugar (6S), raised marks; creamer, 4 1/2" by 4 1/4" by 2 7/8"; sugar, 5 1/8" by 4 3/4" by 2 1/2". **$150-$170/pair**

Freesia blue basket (390-7"), 8 1/4" by 7 3/8" by 3 5/8". **$300-$350**

Freesia blue hanging basket, minor glaze scaling to a few high points, stamped USA, 5 1/2" by 7 3/4". **$150-$175**

Two Freesia pieces: blue basket (392-10") with restored chip at base, and brown flowerpot (670-5"), raised marks. **$125-$175/pair**

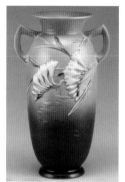

Freesia brown lamp base and fittings, bruise to one handle, no visible mark; pottery: 13" tall.
$400-$450

Freesia brown bulbous vase (128-15"), restoration to rim, raised mark.
if perfect $350-$400
otherwise $175-$225

Freesia brown two-handled vase (125-10"), raised mark, 10 1/4" by 5 3/4".
$175-$225

Freesia brown flaring two-handled vase (122-8"), raised mark, 8 1/4" by 5 5/8".   **$225-$250**

Freesia brown flaring two-handled vase (124-9"), base chip, 9 1/2" by 7 3/8" by 4 5/8".
$300-$350

Freesia brown two-handled vase with bulbous base (126-10"), raised mark, 10 1/4" by 6 1/4".
$125-$150

Freesia brown bulbous vase (463-5"), raised mark, 5 1/8" by 8 1/4" by 7".   **$100-$125**

Left: Four Freesia pieces: green bud vase (195-7") with two small glaze misses to neck, green pillow vase (199-6"), and a pair of brown book-shaped bookends (15) with restoration to edges on both, raised marks.
$250-$300/set

Freesia green cookie jar (4-8"), several small chips on bottom ring, raised mark. **$275-$300**

Freesia green tall ewer (21-15"), firing line to rim, two 1/2" chips to base, raised mark. **$250-$300**

Freesia green jardinière (669-8") with some glaze nicks to rim, raised mark. **$200-$250**

Two Freesia green pieces: urn (127-12") and two-handled vase (121-8"), raised marks. **$350-$400/pair**

Three Freesia green pieces: pitcher (20-10") with flat chip to base, small bowl (464-6"), and center bowl (467-10") with 1/4" chip and fleck to rim, all marked. **$225-$275/set**

Left: Three Freesia pieces: green planter (669-4") with chip to one handle, green pillow vase (199-6"), and blue cornucopia-shaped vase (198-8"), all marked. **$200-$250/set**

Fuchsia

A strikingly simple design, Fuchsia (1938) features small hanging flowers and large heart-shaped leaves on backgrounds that are both smooth and textured. Most collectors refer to the colors simply as blue, brown, and green, but the body colors vary from amber-pink-brown to blue-white, to a mix of olive and forest green shot with dark salmon tones. Pieces usually have impressed marks.

Fuchsia blue floor vase (905-18") with crisp mold, impressed mark. **$900-$1,000**

Fuchsia blue water pitcher with ice lip (1322), impressed mark, 8".
$400-$500

Fuchsia blue console set (351-10" and 113-2") with strong mold and color, 1" bruise to bowl, impressed marks.
$375-$400/set

Fuchsia blue center bowl (353-14"), impressed mark.
$225-$275

Fuchsia blue vase (903-12") with strong mold and color, impressed mark.
$450-$550

Fuchsia blue hanging basket with three handles, unmarked, 5 1/2" by 6 1/2". **$350-$375**

Fuchsia blue flowerpot with under plate (646-5"), under plate may not match, minor glaze scale to one flower, impressed mark. **$300-$325**

Fuchsia blue wall pocket (1282-8"), raised mark.
$600-$700

Fuchsia brown pitcher (1322), peppering to body, impressed mark, 8" by 8 1/2". **$350-$400**

Fuchsia brown basket (350-8") with attached flower frog, impressed mark. **$275-$325**

Fuchsia brown bulbous vase, minute pock mark and shallow spider line to base does not go through, obscured impressed mark, 8 1/4" by 6". **$110-$140**

Fuchsia brown jardinière with crisp mold and good color, unmarked, 6 3/4" by 9 1/2". **$150-$200**

Fuchsia brown console set (1133-5" and 350-8"), impressed marks. **$325-$375/set**

Fuchsia green vase (904-15") with good mold and color, impressed mark. **$650-$750**

Fuchsia green center bowl (350-8"), hairline through base and minute fleck to one handle, impressed mark. **$90-$110**

Fuchsia green bulbous vase, faint impressed mark, 8 1/2" by 6 1/2". **$110-$140**

Fuchsia green bulbous pitcher (1322), several flecks overall and restoration to rim, impressed mark, 9" by 8 1/2". **$200-$250**

Fuchsia green bulbous vase (898-8"), minor abrasion at rim, raised mark. **$150-$200**

Fuchsia green bulbous vase (34-7"), minor peppering near rim, impressed mark. **$150-$200**

Fuchsia green flaring two-handled vessel, obscured impressed mark, 6 1/2" by 5 1/2". **$110-$140**

Fuchsia green bulbous vase (illegible mark) with 1/2" tight line to rim, impressed mark. **$275-$300**

Fudji

Unlike Fujiyama and Woodland, which were also the creations of Gazo Foudji, this pattern from the first decade of the 20th century has symmetrical, stylized art nouveau patterns—with suggestions of Persian influence—on similarly shaped vessels, and Rozane Ware wafers.

Fudji four-sided and twisted vase (shape R 5), Rozane Ware wafer, 9 3/4" tall. **$2,800-$3,200**

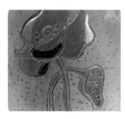

Fujiyama/Woodland

Designed by Gazo Fujiyama, the wares are closely related to Woodland. Introduced in 1905-06, these pieces have delicate glazed floral motifs on a textured, buff-colored body. The Fujiyama pieces have an ink stamp, while Woodland pieces have a Rozane/Woodland wafer. Fujiyama should not be confused with Fudji, which has symmetrical, stylized art nouveau patterns on similarly shaped vessels, plus Rozane Ware wafers.

Woodland four-sided vase decorated with mistletoe, Rozane Woodland wafer, 8 3/4". **$800-$900**

Fujiyama cylindrical vase with brown daylilies, restoration to some small areas of enamel, Fujiyama ink stamp, 15" by 4". **$1,800-$2,000**

Woodland vase with naturalistic floral motif, shape W-974, Rozane Ware Woodland wafer, 10 1/2" tall. **$750-$850**

Woodland corseted vase, enamel-decorated with white blossoms and green leaves, restoration to chip at rim, Rozane Ware/Woodland wafer, 10" by 3". **$475-$525**

Woodland four-sided vase decorated with brown flowers and stylized leaves, fleck and very short, tight line to rim, minor flat chips at base, marked "ROZANE WARE," 8 3/4" by 2 1/2". **$250-$300**

Woodland bulbous vase, decorated with glossy brown poppies and leaves on an ivory bisque base, 1/2" chip at base, line inside rim does not go through, and slight firing burst to one petal, marked "Rozane Ware Woodland," incised "ED," and "ET" written along base, 16 1/4" by 6". **$1,100-$1,300**

Far left: Fujiyama bud vase decorated with a poppy, 1/2" chip and glaze flakes to base, marked Fujiyama, 5 1/4" tall. **$375-$425**
Left: Fujiyama classically shaped vase decorated with white blossoms, glaze flaking to top and bottom, hairline to rim, Fujiyama ink stamp, 8 1/2" by 4 1/4". **$325-$375**

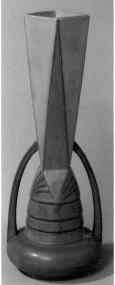

Futura

Futura is a striking blend of art deco and floral designs, both naturalistic and stylized. Introduced in 1924, everything was fair game, and previously unknown colors, shapes, and glaze combinations continue to emerge. Pieces are unmarked or have a black paper label.

Below: Futura faceted pedestal vase (412-9", known as "The Tank"), in streaked tan over blue, unmarked, 9 1/2" by 8 3/4". **$14,000-$15,000**
Below left: Futura vase with squat base, two handles, and a flaring faceted top in orange, brown, and blue-green, unmarked, 14 1/2" by 5 1/4". **$2,500-$3,500**

Futura chalice in two shades of glossy green, restoration to stilt-pull chip, 2" hairline from rim, black paper label, very rare, 5 3/4" by 3 1/2". **$1,400-$1,600**

Futura spherical vessel on trapezoidal base with polychrome circles on a green ground, 1/4" bruise to rim, unmarked, 8 1/4" by 6 1/2". **$900-$1,000**

Futura two-handled vase with bulbous base and stacked neck, covered in a bright green and charcoal semi-matte glaze, unmarked, 9" by 5". **$800-$900**

Futura conical vase with three buttresses in orange and green, unmarked, 8" by 5". **$650-$750**

Futura four-sided vase (#402) in orange and blue with green buttresses to each corner, some tiny nicks to edges, unmarked, 8 1/4" by 3 3/4". **$600-$700**

Futura four-sided vase (#402) with green buttresses on a pale blue to beige ground, 1/2" tight line to rim and 1/4" chip to bottom of one buttress, unmarked, 8" by 3 3/4". **$500-$600**

Futura faceted center bowl with blossoms, the interior covered in an orange glaze, the exterior in mottled blue, minor glaze miss to rim, unmarked, 3 3/4" by 12".
$500-$600

Futura swollen four-sided footed vessel with stylized art deco flowers, 1/2" glaze miss to edge, unmarked, 9 1/2" by 5".
$850-$950

Futura bottle-shaped vase with stepped neck in green and brown, several chips to base, remnant of black paper label, 9" by 8".
$475-$525

Futura four-sided flaring vessel on a buttressed base, both covered in a mottled green and umber glaze, opposing lines to rim, cracks to two buttresses, chip and several flecks to base, unmarked, 4 1/4" by 5".
$250-$300

Futura jardinière and pedestal with pastel leaves on an orange ground, small burst to shoulder and spider lines to base of jardinière; restoration around rim, touch-ups, 3 1/2" line to base, and flat chip to bottom of pedestal, unmarked; jardinière: 10" by 15"; pedestal: 18 1/2" by 11 1/4".
$400-$500

Pair of Futura candlesticks with orange, green, and blue geometric pattern, one has small chip to base, black label, 4" by 3 1/4".
$650-$750

Futura beehive-shaped vessel in blue and amber glazes, two minor chips inside foot ring, unmarked, 7 1/4" by 5 3/4".
$400-$500

Two Futura pieces: small vase with squat base in orange and green and flat vase in pink with stylized flowers, black paper label to first, 7 1/2" by 4 1/2" and 4 1/4" by 6 1/2".
$500-$600/pair

Futura vase with buttressed handles decorated with tulips on a blue, green, and yellow mottled ground, colored-in chip and repair to base, touch-ups to several small glaze chips around rim, and spider lines to base that go up side of vase, unmarked, 13" by 6 1/4".
$400-$500

Futura twisted four-sided vase with branches and leaves on a mottled orange to green ground, small clay pimple or kiln mark to one corner and Y-shaped line, unmarked, 6 1/2" by 3". **$225-$275**

Right: Futura jardinière decorated with spade-shaped leaves, unmarked, 7" by 10 1/2". **$400-$450**

Futura ovoid vessel with branches and blue blossoms, unmarked, 8 1/2" by 5 1/4". **$1,000-$1,200**

Gardenia

Introduced in 1950, Gardenia features a wide belt of white blossoms and green leaves evenly wrapped around the vessels. Background colors are tan-brown with an orange tinge, gray, and shades of green. Pieces feature raised marks.

Below: Two Gardenia brown vases: one flaring, (687-12") and one bulbous (688-12") with repair to chips at base, raised marks. **$200-$250/pair**
Below left: Gardenia brown ewer (618-15"), raised mark. **$300-$350**

Gardenia brown ewer (616-6"), raised mark, 6 1/4" by 3" by 3". **$175-$225**

Two Gardenia brown pieces: double bud vase (622-8") and basket (608-8"), raised marks. **$200-$225/pair**

Gardenia green basket (609-10"), raised mark. **$300-$350**

Two Gardenia vases: green bulbous (684-8") with chip to one petal and under-glaze chip at base, and brown ovoid (682-5"), both marked. **$350-$400/pair**

Three Gardenia pieces: brown cornucopia-shaped vase (621-6"), green bulbous vase (685-10"), and long brown bowl (630-12") with fleck to one edge of rim, raised marks. **$200-$250/set**

Gardenia green window box (658-8"), raised mark, 8 3/4" by 3 1/8" by 3 1/8". **$125-$150**

Gardenia gray hanging basket, good mold, short, tight 1" line from rim, stamped USA, 5 1/4" by 7 3/4".   **$90-$110**

Four Gardenia gray pieces: jardinière (641-5"), double vase (622-8"), and a pair of candlesticks (652-4 1/2"), all marked.   **$225-$275/set**

Gardenia gray vase (689-14"), raised mark.
                $250-$300

Two Gardenia pieces: gray vase (683-8") and green spherical planter (641-5"), glaze flake to handle of planter, raised marks.   **$200-$225/pair**

Two Gardenia pitchers: one green (617-10"), one gray (616-6"), raised marks.   **$175-$200/pair**

Left: Pair of Gardenia gray double vases (622-8"), raised marks.
                $150-$200/pair

German Cookware

Dating from about the turn of the 19th century, these wares in simple brown glazes were produced for the Romafin Pottery Co. of Chicago. Pieces also included bowls, covered casseroles, long-handled pots, and platters. All are unmarked.

German Cookware, all unmarked.
Teapot, 7 1/4" tall with lid	$250-$300
Coffeepot, 8 1/2" tall with lid	$300-$350
Creamer, 3 1/4" tall.	$40-$50

Hexagon

From 1924, Hexagon was part of the Rosecraft line and has broad faceted shapes with an Arts & Crafts-inspired decoration. It is commonly brown and green, and rarely black or blue. It has an "Rv" ink stamp or label.

Two Hexagon vases, both with "Rv" ink stamp: 266-4" in brown, **$100-$125**; 270-8" in dull green. **$600-$700**

Rosecraft Hexagon green double bud vase in gate form (45-5"), "Rv" ink stamp, 5 1/4" tall. **$550-$600**; Rosecraft Hexagon low bowl in green (135-5"), "Rv" ink stamp, 2 3/8" tall. **$225-$250**

Hexagon green wall pocket, touch-up to glaze chips on back, small bruise to edge, "Rv" ink stamp, 8 1/2" tall.
$400-$450

Rosecraft Hexagon vase (8-7"), "Rv" ink stamp, 7 3/8" tall. **$350-$400**; Rosecraft Hexagon candlestick, "Rv" ink stamp, 8 1/8" tall. **$150-$200**

Pair of Hexagon brown vases, 1/2" hairline to rim and some minute flecks to base of one, restoration to hairline and chip at rim of other, "Rv" ink stamp, 4 1/2" by 6 1/2" each.
$275-$325/pair

Hexagon green vase, 1" line from rim and flake to base, "Rv" ink stamp, 4 1/4". **$200-$250**

Home Art

Introduced before 1910, and as the name implies, Home Art was Roseville's do-it-yourself line. Pieces could be hand-painted or have transfer decoration from the factory. Most pieces are unmarked, and very few survive.

Above: Home Art three-footed jardinière painted with tulips on a teal and ivory ground, repaired chip inside rim, pock mark outside rim, and glaze chip to foot, unmarked, rare, 10" by 12". **$325-$375**
Left: Home Art flower pot, painted with flower, unmarked, 3 1/2" tall. **$125-$150**

Hyde Park

Roseville made ashtrays and cigarette boxes for the Hyde Park Company, which then resold the items for use as presentation pieces in the late 1940s and early '50s. The ashtrays have an ap plied copper-colored metal disk with a raised initial. Marks include "The Hyde Park," and a style number or year.

Below: Three Hyde Park monogrammed ashtrays, one triangular and two biomorphic, several nicks overall, each marked "The Hyde Park - U.S.A."; largest: 10 1/2" long.   **$80-$90/set**
Left: Two Hyde Park monogrammed ashtrays, one yellow and one beige, both marked, 9" diameter each.
$80-$90/pair

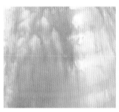

Imperial I and II

There is no confusing Imperial I with Imperial II. Though both were introduced late in the first quarter of the 20th century, Imperial I has a rustic appearance, with a rough textured surface that mixes muddy green, brown, and ivory, and a stylized grape vine that has an odd pretzel-like appearance. This motif is set off by a shamrock-shaped leaf and a blue-gray blob that suggests a grape cluster, but you really have to use your imagination to see any grapes. Pieces are unmarked.

Imperial II is the later version, and many of the vessels have striking color combinations, like yellow-lavender, turquoise-pink, orange-green, or mottled amber and raspberry, often dripping or blurred together. Pieces are mostly unmarked but occasionally have paper labels.

Imperial II low bowl covered in a mottled orange glaze, unmarked, 8 1/2" diameter.   **$350-$400**

Imperial I bulbous vase, unmarked, 10" by 8".
$250-$300

Imperial I basket, unmarked, 6" by 7".
$175-$225

Imperial I basket, unmarked, 10 1/4" by 6".
$150-$200

Imperial I footed vessel with closed-in rim, 1/4" glaze pimple to body, unmarked, 12" by 6 1/4".
$225-$250

Imperial I triple vase (29-8"), 7 5/8" by 4 3/4" by 3 1/2". **$300**

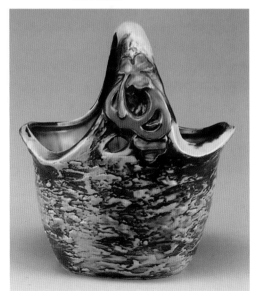

Imperial I basket, minor fleck at edge of base, unmarked, 10 3/4" by 10". **$175-$225**

Imperial II wall pocket with mottled pink and green semi-matte glaze, black paper label, 6 1/2" tall. **$900-$1,000**

Imperial II bulbous vessel with ribbed body, covered in a purple and yellow mottled glaze, unmarked, 6 1/4" by 6". **$500-$600**

Imperial II wall pocket covered in a mottled greenish-gold and magenta glaze, "Rv" ink stamp, 7 1/4" tall. **$350-$400**

Imperial II shouldered vessel covered in a frothy turquoise glaze with yellow design around rim, black paper label, 7 1/4" by 7 1/2". **$500-$600**

Imperial II triple wall pocket covered in a mottled green and gold glaze, short, tight line on edge of center holder, unmarked, 6 1/2" tall. **$250-$350**

Imperial II beehive-shaped vase in yellow and lavender, short tight line to rim, unmarked, 6" by 5 3/4". **$200-$250**

Imperial II squat vessel with embossed collar rim and green and purple mottled glaze, unmarked, 4 1/2" by 6 1/4". **$300-$350**

Left: Imperial II tapering vase with ribbed band to body, minute fleck to body, unmarked, 5 1/4" by 3 1/4".

$125-$175

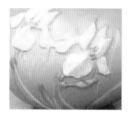

Iris

Another design that faithfully mimics nature, Iris (1939) features pairs of large blossoms and tall, slender leaves. Backgrounds are the familiar blue-turquoise, salmon-brown, and dusty pink. Pieces usually feature impressed marks, but they are sometimes unmarked.

Iris brown jardinière (647-10") and pedestal set, small reglued chip to pedestal, nick to rim, and small filled-in chips to flowers on jardinière, both marked.

$900-$1,000

Iris brown bulbous vase with flaring rim (920-7"), impressed mark.
$110-$140

Iris brown flaring footed urn with squat base (823-8"), minor bruise to one corner of handle, impressed mark. **$175-$200**

Right: Iris blue center or console bowl (362-10"), impressed mark, 12 5/8" by 6 3/4" by 3 7/8".
$175-$225

Two Iris brown pieces: footed pillow vase (922-8") with 1 1/2" chip to base and oval basket planter (355-10"), impressed marks. **$400-$450/pair**

Two Iris brown pieces: cornucopia vase (134-6") and small footed vessel with squat base (130-4"), very faint impressed mark to one. **$175-$200/pair**

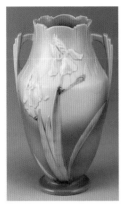

Iris blue bulbous vase (929-15"), impressed mark. **$750-$850**

Iris blue wall shelf (2), minute and shallow bruise to one side of shelf, impressed mark, 8 1/4" by 5". **$450-$500**

Iris blue flaring vase with bulbous base, illegible impressed mark, 10 1/2" by 7 1/2". **$350-$400**

Two Iris blue pieces: fan vase (922-8") and cornucopia vase (132-8"), impressed marks. **$375-$400/pair**

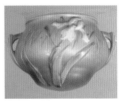

Iris blue hanging basket with two handles, some abrasion to bottom, unmarked, 5 1/4" by 8 1/2". **$275-$300**

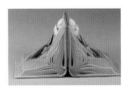

Iris blue bookends (5), fleck to tip of one, raised marks, 5 1/4" by 5". **$125-$175/pair**

Iris blue flowerpot with under plate (648-5"), 1" bruise to rim of pot, raised marks. **$275-$300**

Iris blue footed basket planter (355-10"), restoration to handle on one side, impressed mark. **$150-$175**

Iris pink bulbous urn (928-12"), impressed mark.
$400-$450

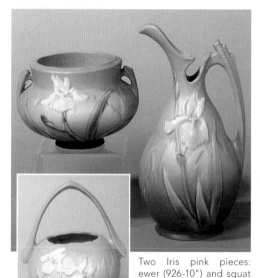

Two Iris pink pieces: ewer (926-10") and squat planter (647-4") with minor bruise to one petal, impressed marks.
$350-$400/pair

Iris pink spherical basket planter (354-8"), impressed mark.**$250-$300**

Iris pink ovoid footed vase (924-9"), strong mold and good glazing, impressed mark. **$275-$300**

Right: Iris pink console set with oval center bowl (360-10") and a pair of candlesticks (1135-4 1/2"), impressed marks.
$300-$350/set

Ivory (Old)

Dating from the first decade of the 20th century, the Old Ivory line features geometric patterns, and floral motifs both stylized and naturalistic, on creamy-colored vessels—most often jardinières—with dark backgrounds of brown or tan. Unmarked, or with paper labels.

Ivory (Tinted)

An atypical design for the Roseville creamwares, Tinted Ivory features Greek Key patterns and scrolls on a group of teapots, creamers, and sugar bowls, plus floral bands on tall tankards and mugs, and even smoker sets. Bisque vessels are accented with colors that include pale yellow, blue, green, and pink. All are unmarked.

Left: Old Ivory jardinière with leafy and floral motif (503), impressed mark, 7 3/4" tall. **$350-$450**

Tinted Ivory footed planter and liner; unmarked planter is 4" tall, liner (shape 515) is 3" tall. **$250-$300**

Tinted Ivory double bud vase in gate form, unmarked, 5" tall by 6 3/4" wide, $200-$250; and a teapot, unmarked, 4 3/8" tall. **$100-$125**

Ivory

Sometimes called Ivory II to distinguish it from the Old Ivory and Ivory Tint of 1910-12, this line from 1932 featured unadorned white vessels made in the molds of other patterns, including Donatello, Carnelian I, Foxglove, and Luffa, to name just a few. The markings vary, and some pieces have labels.

Nine Ivory II pieces including several vases and a basket, some chips, but overall excellent condition, some marked. **$400-$450/set**

Seven Ivory II pieces: low bowl (152-6") with bruise to base; flaring vase (260-8") on Russco blank (repairs); larger flaring bowl on Russco blank (cracks); small planter; tall vase on Savona blank (flecks to base); bowl (266-6") on Velmoss blank (cracks and chips); and cornucopia vase (106-7") with flat chip to base.

$110-$140/set

Ivory II ewer vase in a Carnelian I shape (1315-15"), 15" by 8 1/8" by 5 3/4".

$400-$500

Seven Ivory II candlesticks: two on faceted bases, three spherical, and two tall, one of which has an unusual blue-glazed rim, some marked.

$150-$200/set

Five Ivory II pieces: squat planter (several hairlines, probably in firing); flaring 9" vase; small vase; large bulbous vase (chip to handle); and smaller bulbous vase, some impressed marks, large bulbous vase: 8 1/2" tall.

$150-$200/set

Ixia

Victorian gardeners associated the Ixia with happiness, and this line from 1937 reflects the company's robust business as the country emerged from the Depression (Roseville sales and production peaked just a few years later). The stylized bloss oms seem to be blowing in the wind on backgrounds of green, pink-green, and yellow-brown. Marks are impressed.

Two Ixia green pieces with buttressed handles: hemispheric bowl (325-5") with 1/4" chip to one handle and ovoid vase (855-7") with crisp mold (minute fleck to rim), impressed marks. **$125-$150/pair**

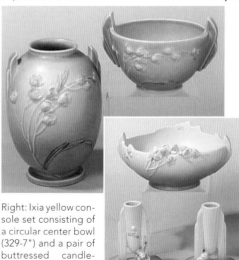

Ixia green vase (064-12"), some peppering to body, impressed mark, and remnant of foil label to body. **$110-$140**

Right: Ixia yellow console set consisting of a circular center bowl (329-7") and a pair of buttressed candlesticks (1126-4 1/4"), impressed marks. **$175-$200/set**

Above: Two Ixia yellow pieces: small planter (illegible mark) and footed vase with two buttressed supports (861-10"), impressed marks; planter: 4 1/2" by 4 1/2". **$300-$350/pair**

Two Ixia pink buttressed pieces with crisp mold: vase (856-8") with peppering throughout and flowerpot (64-5") without under plate (minor flake to corner of one buttress), impressed marks.

$150-$200/pair

Ixia yellow combination planter and candlestick holder (328) with minor flecks to rim and base, impressed mark, 4 1/4" by 12 1/4". **$250-$300**

Two Ixia yellow vases: one flaring (854-7") and one ovoid (853-6"), one minute burst to each, impressed marks.

$375-$400/pair

Two Ixia pink vases: one with collared rim (illegible mark) and one flaring (852-6"), both have crisp molds, impressed marks; taller: 10 1/2" by 4 3/4".

$275-$325/pair

Jonquil

Introduced about 1931, Jonquil has trios of flowers girdling a textured body that has a color transition of mottled brown and ivory moving up to muddy brown and green. The interiors are usually glazed in a brighter variegated green. Pieces are unmarked with silver foil labels.

Jonquil strawberry planter with attached under plate, unmarked, rare, 6 1/4" by 8 1/2". **$800-$900**

Jonquil flaring wall pocket, silver foil tag, 8" tall.
$650-$750

Jonquil console set, stilt-pull chip to bowl, silver foil label on candlesticks; candlesticks: 4 1/4" by 4 1/4"; bowl: 3 3/4" by 12".
$500-$600

Jonquil bulbous vase with crisp mold, professionally restored 1/2" chip at rim, some minor nicks at base, unmarked, 12 1/4" tall.
$450-$550

Jonquil gourd-shaped vase, bruise to one flower, pinhead-sized fleck to rim, unmarked, 8 1/4" by 5 1/2".
$325-$375

Jonquil bulbous vase with flaring rim, burst bubbles to base, unmarked, 9 1/2" by 6 1/4".
$350-$400

Left: Pair of Jonquil candlesticks, unmarked, 4 1/4" tall each.
$650-$750/pair

Jonquil basket, paper label, rare, 8 1/2" by 5 1/2".
$350-$450

Jonquil flaring center bowl with built-in flower frog, strong mold, unmarked, rare, 10 1/2" diameter.
$400-$500

Jonquil flaring vase, black paper label, 7 1/4" by 4 1/2". **$300-$375**

Jonquil bulbous vase, unmarked, 8 1/4" by 7 1/4".
$300-$375

Jonquil jardinière, spider lines to base (lines go through), minor nicks to high points, unmarked, 9" by 11". **$275-$325**

Right: Jonquil bulbous vase with crisp mold, unmarked, 6" by 7".
$250-$300
Far right: Jonquil bulbous handled vase, unmarked, 8" by 6 7/8" by 6 7/8".
$550-$650

Two Jonquil pieces: spherical vase and small bowl, unmarked, 4" tall and 4 1/4" tall. **$325-$375/pair**

Jonquil bulbous vase, unmarked, 6 3/4" by 7 1/4". **$225-$275**

Jonquil spherical vase, unmarked, 5" tall. **$225-$275**

Jonquil bulbous vase, nick to one flower, unmarked, 6 1/4" by 5 3/4". **$200-$250**

Jonquil jardinière, several nicks overall, 3/4" chip to one handle, unmarked, 9" by 12 1/2". **$225-$275**

Jonquil bulbous vase, 2" line from rim, unmarked, 4 1/4" by 6 1/4". **$125-$175**

Jonquil squat vessel, small stilt-pull chips, unmarked, 4" by 4 1/2". **$125-$175**

Jonquil flaring vase, unmarked, 7" by 5". **$175-$225**

Juvenile

Considered part of the creamwares, the Juvenile pieces have bright bands of color and transfer decorations of playful animals and children. There is also a rare Santa Claus motif. Most pieces are unmarked, but occasionally have an "Rv" ink stamp.

Three-piece Juvenile set painted with rabbits ("ears down") and a green stripe, consisting of a cereal bowl (No. 13), creamer (No. 13), and sugar (No. 6), "Rv" ink stamps, bowl: 6" diameter. **$900-$1,000/set**

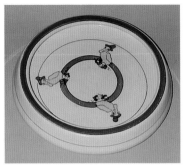

Juvenile dish with duck in boots and hat, some losses to enamel, "Rv" ink stamp, 7 3/4" diameter. **$65-$75**

Three-piece Juvenile set painted with chicks: cup, saucer, and small plate, some light wear to decoration, unmarked; plate: 6 1/2" diameter. **$225-$275/set**

Two Juvenile pieces: bowl with girls in bonnets (several chips to rim) and mug with ducks (hairline to rim), "Rv" ink stamps to both; bowl: 5 1/4" diameter. **$80-$100/pair**

Juvenile mug painted with rabbits, minute fleck, several bruises (in firing), hairline, unmarked, 3" by 3 3/4". **$110-$140**

Juvenile dish and cup painted with rabbits, several minor nicks overall, "Rv" ink stamp to both; bowl: 8" diameter. **$175-$225/pair**

La Rose

Introduced in 1924, La Rose features evenly spaced garland swags and clusters of roses and leaves on a creamy background. Pieces are unmarked or have an "Rv" ink stamp.

Above:
 La Rose low bowl (127-7")
$125-$150
Candleholder (1051-4")
$200-$250
Both with "Rv" ink stamps.

La Rose wall pocket (1233-7"), "Rv" ink stamp.
$400-$450

Three La Rose vessels: low bowl with crisp mold and burst clay bubbles, double bud vase, and ovoid vase with 1/2" bruise to rim; two have "Rv" ink stamp; bowl: 9" diameter; vases: 4 1/4" by 9", and 6 1/4" tall.
$300-$350/set

Landscape

Part of the creamwares made about 1915, this decoration is frequently found on tea sets, and pots for coffee or chocolate. It may also picture a woodland stream in brown or blue on white. These pieces are unmarked, and are often heavily crazed.

Landscape teapot, creamer, and sugar set with transfer seascapes in blue. **$300-$350**

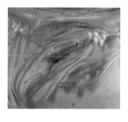

Laurel

A mix of nature and art deco, Laurel (1934) features tapering leaves and berries draped over panels of three vertical grooves. Dripping glazes cover bodies of ochre, mottled orange-red, and dusty green, but other color combinations continue to be found. Pieces are unmarked or have gold foil labels.

Trial glaze Laurel vase with two low buttressed handles, covered in a dark brown and rich amber glaze, gold foil label, 12 1/4" by 8". **$1,100**

Laurel green bulbous vase with collared rim, unmarked, 6" by 3 3/4".
$275-$325

Laurel yellow ovoid vase, unmarked, 6" by 3 1/2".
$200-$250

Laurel red vase with buttressed handles, foil label, and remnant of store label, 7 1/2" by 5".
$225-$275

Laurel red vase with buttressed handles, nick and 1/2" chip to base, gold foil label, 8" by 6 1/2".
$110-$140

Laurel yellow flaring vase, unmarked, 10 1/4" tall.
$450-$500

Laurel yellow console set: center bowl and a pair of candlesticks, line to one candlestick, chips to the other, foil label on one; bowl: 4" by 9 1/2". **$300-$350/set**

Left: Laurel green vessel with abrasion around rim and flake to rib, unmarked, 6 1/2" by 7".
$225-$275

Lombardy

The bulbous reeded design of Lombardy was introduced in 1924. The finish can be dull or glossy, and the colors are mostly solid blues and greens. Pieces are unmarked.

Lombardy wall pocket covered in a blue-gray glossy glaze, unmarked, 9" tall. **$250-$300**

Right: Lombardy wall pocket in a gray-blue matte glaze, unmarked, 9 1/2" tall. **$250-$300**

Lombardy dark green hanging basket with abrasion to bottom, unmarked, 7 3/4" wide. **$150-$200**

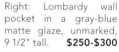

Lombardy wall pocket covered in a blue-gray glossy glaze, unmarked, 9" tall. **$250-$300**

Two Lombardy pieces: green small dish with bruise to rim, and blue vase, black paper label on one, 2" by 5 1/2" and 6 1/2" by 4". **$90-$110/pair**

Lotus

Introduced near the end of the company's existence in 1951, Lotus features a tight "picket fence" of leaves, usually in ivory or yellow, banded on the top and bottom by colors that included blue, green, red, brown, and yellow. Pieces are distinctly marked with "Lotus" and a style number/size.

Above: Two Lotus pieces, one red vase (L3-10") and a square brown planter (L9-4") with minor firing bruise to one corner of base, raised marks. **$150-$200/pair**

Inset above right: Lotus green wall pocket (L8-7") with a very short inner firing line, raised mark. **$550-$600**

Lotus tapering vase (L3-10") covered in a glossy sky blue and beige trial glaze, raised mark and glaze codes to bottom. **$800-$900**

Right: Two Lotus rectangular planters, one green and one blue (L7-10 1/2"), raised marks.
$350-$400/pair

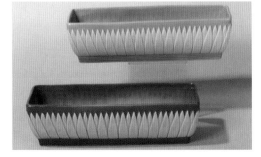

Luffa

From 1934, Luffa features small yellow or white flowers and large green leaves on a wavy ridged surface. Background colors are dominant green with brown accents, or dominant brown with variegated green accents. Pieces are unmarked or have foil labels.

Luffa green ovoid vase with collared rim, some peppering to rim and bruise to base, unmarked, 8 1/4" by 5 1/4". **$175-$225**

Luffa brown console set consisting of a four-sided center bowl with scalloped rim (underglaze bruise to rim) and a pair of short candlesticks (good mold, one has small fleck and touch-up to 1/4" rim chip, other has minor burst bubble to rim), unmarked; bowl: 3 3/4" by 13 1/4", sticks: 5" tall. **$225-$275/set**

Luffa green wall pocket, unmarked, 8 1/4".
$650-$750

Luffa green tapering footed vase, strong mold and good color, unmarked, 14 1/2" by 9 3/4".
$750-$850

Luffa green tapering vase, unmarked, 6" by 4".
$175-$225

Luffa green bulbous vessel, unmarked, 6 1/2" by 6 1/2".
$400-$450

Luffa green bowl, unmarked, 4" by 10".
$275-$325

Luffa brown planter, unmarked, 5" by 7".
$150-$200

Luffa brown bulbous jardinière, 2" hairline from rim, unmarked, 6 1/2" by 6 1/2". **$150-$200**

Two Luffa pieces: green planter with small repaired chips to base and brown bulbous vase with small nick to base, foil label on planter; 5" and 6" tall.
$325-$375/pair

Two Luffa vases: one brown ovoid (good mold, 2" hairline from rim) and one green with flaring rim (1/2" bruise to rim), unmarked; 7 1/2" by 4 1/2" and 7 1/4" by 4 3/4".　　　**$275-$325/pair**

Two Luffa green vases: each with collared rim (one is sea foam green, the other emerald green), unmarked, 6 1/4" by 3 3/4" each.　　　**$400-$450/pair**

Two Luffa pieces: brown rectangular footed bowl and green tapering vase, unmarked; 4 1/4" by 9 1/2" and 6 1/2" by 4 1/2".　　　**$250-$300/pair**

Two Luffa brown vases: one with collared rim, the other cylindrical, unmarked, 6 1/4" and 6 1/2" tall.　**$275-$325/pair**

Lustre

Introduced in 1921 or '22, Lustre also borrowed from Rosecraft shapes and offered the high-gloss colors of azure, blue, pink, orange, and yellow. Pieces are unmarked or have a paper label.

Left: Three tall Lustre candlesticks: pair of orange (one minor fleck to each, a few insignificant color scratches, one has short line to base) and single ivory (shallow 2 in. hairline to base), all unmarked, each approximately 10" tall.
$150-$200/set
Below: Two Lustre baskets in glossy pink: left, 297, 7 1/2", unmarked. **$300-$350**; right, 299, 9", black paper label. **$350-$400**

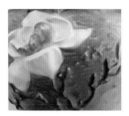

Magnolia

Though the magnolia is the most ancient of flowering plants, Roseville didn't introduce this line until very late in its existence—1943. It's also not clear what species this is (there are about 75), since magnolias typically have a single center receptacle, and the pottery flowers appear to have several. The large blooms on gnarled black branches can be found on backgrounds of blue with brown and amber-green accents, orange-brown with green accents, and green with brown-yellow accents. Pieces feature raised marks.

Three Magnolia pieces: pair of blue vases (87-6"), one with nick to base, and vase (92-8") with nick to one branch, all marked.   **$175-$225/set**

Magnolia blue ewer (15-15"), minor peppering overall and 1/2" glaze miss to base, raised mark. **$300-$350**

Five Magnolia blue pieces: water pitcher with cracked handle, large vase with chips, ewer with reglued spout, single low candlestick, and rectangular planter, all marked. **$225-$275/set**

Magnolia blue bulbous vase (96-12"), raised mark. **$110-$140**

Six Magnolia pieces: blue cornucopia vase (184-6"), brown bowl (448-8"), pair of blue candlesticks (1157-4 1/2"), blue sugar dish (4-S), and brown rectangular planter (389-8"), raised marks. **$275-$325/set**

Pair of Magnolia blue bookends (13), restoration to one corner, 5 1/4" by 5 1/4" by 5 3/4". **$110-$140/pair**

Left: Magnolia blue cookie jar (2-8"), a couple of small chips, bruises, and burst bubbles, raised mark. **$125-$175**

Below: Three Magnolia brown pieces: planter (183-6"), candlestick (1157-4 1/2"), and vase (181-8") with restoration to base, all marked. **$150-$200/set**

Above: Three Magnolia brown pieces: shell-shaped planter, basket planter, and bulbous vase (small chips), all marked; tallest: 8". **$200-$250/set**

Below: Two Magnolia green pieces: bulbous vase with chip to flower and Magnolia bowl (448-8") with fleck to one handle and chip to tip of flower at rim, raised marks. **$110-$140/pair**

Above: Three Magnolia green pieces: cornucopia vase (184-6") with small chip to petal, flowerpot (666-5") with hairline and flakes, and center bowl (449-10") with small chips, all marked. **$125-$165/set**

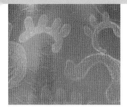

Mara

An iridescent line in the Rozane Wares meant to compete with Weller's Sicardo (also spelled Sicard), Mara (circa 1904) came in forms first created by Roseville a decade earlier. Pieces are rarely marked with a wafer.

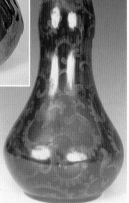

Below: Mara vase (K-22) with contrasting scroll design on a glossy raspberry glaze, faint impressed mark, 8 1/2" tall. **$500-$600**

Above: Mara bulbous tapering vase, unmarked, 8" by 5".
$3,500-$3,700
Courtesy Adamstown Antique Gallery

Mara tapering vase with sprays of flowers and leaves, 2" tight hairline to rim, unmarked, 7 3/4" by 2 1/2". **$300-$400**

Matt Color

This line was introduced about 1920 and featured simple designs, often ribbed, fluted, or with recessed panels. Pieces are unmarked or have foil labels.

Five Matt Color vessels, two spherical and three bulbous, in assorted glazes, unmarked, 3 3/4" by 5 1/2" and 4" by 5 3/4". **$200-$250/set**

Three Matt Color pieces: green and blue hanging basket (bruise to rim of one, glaze flake to other) and blue bowl; two marked; baskets: 4 1/2" by 6 1/2".
$110-$140/set

Above: Four Matt Color squat vessels, in gold, green, blue-green, and royal blue, one has silver foil label, each measures 4" by 7". **$150-$200/set**

Right: Four Matt Color pieces: two vases, one pink and one blue, and two beehive-shaped vessels with short loop handles, one in blue and one in gold; some small burst bubbles; one has foil label; largest: 6 1/4" by 4 1/4". **$150-$200/set**

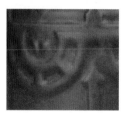

Matt Green

Its name says it all. Introduced about 1910, there were more than 100 styles, mostly planters, jardinières, pedestals, vases, and bowls, both plain and embossed, but they're not easy to find. Pieces are unmarked or have paper labels.

Left: Matt Green footed planter, unmarked, 9" by 10 1/2". **$400-$450**

Matt Green umbrella stand (727 B), unmarked, 20 3/8" tall. **$1,200-$1,500**

Two Matt Green pieces: a flaring vase (shape 5), impressed mark, 9" tall, **$350-$400**; and a flower frog bowl, unmarked, 2 1/2" tall. **$150-$200**

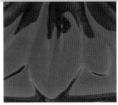

Mayfair

Introduced in the late 1940s, this glossy, colorful line came in both stylized and natural floral motifs on vases, pots, planters, and pitchers. Pieces have raised marks.

Right: Mayfair basket in glossy brown with tan interior (1012-10"), raised mark, 8 1/2" by 10".
$150-$175

Left: Two Mayfair tankard-form pitchers (1107-12"), one green and one brown, both embossed with ferns, raised marks.
$150-$200/pair

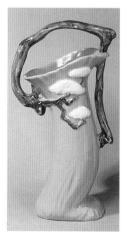

Ming Tree

Although the decoration on this line has been described as a Japanese bonsai tree, "Ming" was one of the Chinese dynasties. Maybe Roseville was trying to cover all the bases with this 1949 introduction. On bodies of glossy Celestial Blue, Jade Green and Temple White, these pieces also have gnarled branches for handles. Pieces have the raised mark, "Roseville U.S.A."

Ming Tree green floor vase (586-15"), raised mark.
$700-$800

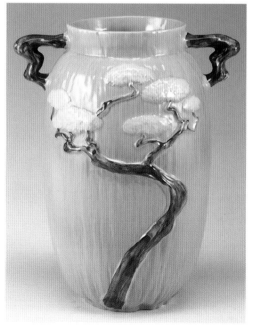

Ming Tree blue vase (510-14"), small flat chip to bottom, raised mark.
$150-$200

Three Ming Tree pieces: tall basket vase (510-14") in ivory with restored crack at base and pair of blue bookends (559), raised marks. **$350-$450/set**

Two Ming Tree green pieces: pitcher (516-10") and two-handled vase (582-8"), raised marks. **$250-$300/pair**

Four Ming Tree pieces: two ashtrays (599), one blue and one green (small bruise to rim of blue one), blue planter (526-9"), and white vase (582-8") with reglued handle, raised marks. **$125-$175/set**

Three Ming Tree blue pieces: pair of low candlesticks (551) and a tall basket vase (510-14") with restoration to rim, raised marks. **$150-$200**

Left: Three Ming Tree blue pieces: pair of bookends (559) with abrasion to back, and tall vase (583-10") with small chips to bottom, raised marks. **$150-$200/pair**

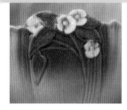

Mock Orange

A throwback to the designs of the 1930s, Mock Orange (1950) featured delicate tiny blossoms on slender stalks, with backgrounds commonly in green, pink, or yellow. The raised mark of "Roseville U.S.A." also included "Mock Orange," or it had a foil label.

Mock Orange green floor vase (986-18") with ruffled rim, raised mark. **$550-$650**

Mock Orange yellow ewer (918-16"), raised mark.
$550-$650

Mock Orange yellow coffee/tea set (971-T, 971-S, 971-C, 971-P), repair to chip on lid of coffee pot, raised marks.
$750-$850/set

Mock Orange yellow jardinière (902-8") and pedestal (905-8"), 1/4" flake to one handle oaf jardinière, some small pockmarks to base of pedestal, raised marks. **$700-$800**

Mock Orange green footed basket (910-10"), restoration where rim and handle meet on one side, raised mark. **$300-$350**

Mock Orange yellow hanging basket, 1/4" glaze inconsistency to rim, stamped "U.S.A.," 5 1/2" by 7 1/4". **$250-$300**

Mock Orange pink vase (985-12") with squat base and flaring rim, repair to 1" section of rim, raised mark. **$125-$175**

Mock Orange pink square pillow vase (92-7"), minor flat chip to one foot, raised mark, 7 1/4" by 7 1/4". **$125-$175**

Three Mock Orange pieces: green jardinière (900-4") and two vases (984-10"), one green and one yellow, raised marks. **$500-$550/set**

Moderne

Introduced at the height of art deco, Moderne (1936) picked up and refined themes introduced two years earlier in Laurel: strong vertical lines juxtaposed with stylized blossoms or tendrils. The plain matt backgrounds include blue, brown, pink, green, and ivory. Most pieces have impressed marks.

Moderne white footed vase (803-14"), restoration to hairline at base, impressed mark. **$250-$300**

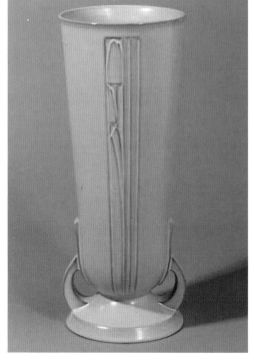

Moderne green chalice (789-6"), impressed mark. **$125-$175**

Left: Two Moderne blue vases: one (802-12") with several chips to base and one to rim, and a tall one with squat base (800-10") with small chip to bottom ring and fleck to corner, impressed marks. **$650-$750/pair**

Moderne blue triple candlestick (1112), line through base, marked, 6" tall. **$150-$200**

Right: Two Moderne white coupe-shaped vases (788-6" and 787-6"), impressed marks and foil label to one. **$250-$300/pair**

Moderne blue console set consisting of an oval center bowl (301-10") and pair of candlesticks (1111-4 1/2"), impressed marks. **$300-$350/set**

Two Moderne pieces: blue urn (787-6") and rust flaring basket, one marked; bowl: 8" diameter. **$325-$375/pair**

Mongol

The glaze that has come to be known as Mongol first received wide recognition in 1904 when the line won first prize at the St. Louis Centennial Exposition. Called oxblood or "sang de boeuf," the blood-red glossy glaze was part of the Rozane line. It would turn other colors if refired, and some pieces have been found with hand-painted decoration, and with silver or gold overlay. Some have a Rozane Ware/Mongol wafer, or paper labels.

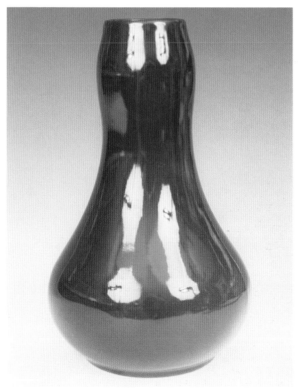

Mongol vase in a Mara shape (K-22), Rozane Ware wafer, 8" tall.
$550-$650

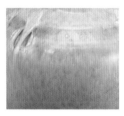

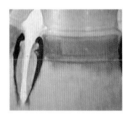

Montacello

Sometimes misspelled Monticello, this line from 1931 has a Southwestern flavor. A collar of watery brown, tan-pink, and green is accented with a modified fleur-de-lis (on some almost an arrowhead shape) in ivory that drips across evenly spaced black ovals. Backgrounds of these heavy-bodied pieces are mottled blue, brown, and green. Pieces are unmarked, or rarely have a silver or black label.

Right: Two Montacello brown vessels: one with flaring rim and one bulbous, unmarked, 5 1/4" by 5" and 5" by 5 3/4". **$600-$700/pair**

Below: Two Montacello vases in mottled glazes:
Left: (560) has a turquoise band, 6 1/4" tall **$550-$650**
Right: (557) has the mottled blue glaze; also has a brown band trimmed in blue, 5" tall. **$400-$450**

Montacello bulbous vase covered in an unusual mottled blue glaze, unmarked, 7 1/2" by 6 1/2". **$600-$700**

Montacello blue bulbous vessel, unmarked, 7 1/4" by 6 1/4". **$550-$650**

Montacello blue ovoid vase, unmarked, 7 1/4" by 5 3/4". **$500-$550**

Montacello blue console set consisting of a faceted center bowl and a pair of candlesticks, very good mold, unmarked; bowl: 3" by 13 1/4", sticks: 5" tall.

$800-$900/set

Two Montacello brown pieces: bulbous vase with flaring rim and corseted vessel, both unmarked, 5 1/4" by 4 1/2" and 4 1/4" by 5". **$400-$450/pair**

Two Montacello blue pieces: vase with flaring rim (1/4" chip to rim) and corseted vessel, both unmarked, 5 1/2" by 5" and 4 1/4" by 5 1/2".

$300-$350/pair

Left: Montacello brown two-handled vase with white fleur-de-lis, unmarked, 4 1/4" by 5".

$300-$350

Montacello brown squat basket with arched handle, unmarked, 6 1/2" by 4 3/4". **$700-$800**

Montacello brown tapering vase, unmarked, 7 1/4" by 5 1/2". **$450-$550**

Montacello brown bulbous vessel, unmarked, 6 1/4" by 7 1/4".
$450-$500

Montacello green urn with fleur-de-lis, unmarked, 9 1/2" by 8" **$800-$900**

Montacello green two-handled corseted vessel, peppering to one side, a couple of small glaze misses to rim, unmarked, 5" tall. **$175-$225**

Montacello green flaring vase, bruise and 1/2" colored-in chip to rim, unmarked, 11" by 6".
$525-$575

Montacello green bulbous vase, unmarked, 7 1/2" by 6". **$450-$500**

Left: Montacello green vase, restoration inside rim and to base, firing line to one handle, light abrasion, unmarked, 9" by 8 1/4". **$350-$400**

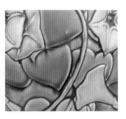

Morning Glory

Introduced in 1935, the appearance of Morning Glory—a looping tangle of flowers, vines, and leaves—owes much to some of the stylized floral patterns found on Ceramic Design pieces of three decades earlier. The lavender, yellow, and pale green palette with dark accents on an ivory or green body is quite distinctive. Pieces are unmarked or feature foil labels.

Morning Glory green bulbous vase, unmarked, 8 1/2" by 6 1/2".   **$900-$1,100**

Morning Glory white buttressed pillow vase, foil label, 7" by 4 3/4".
$300-$350

Morning Glory green flaring vase with strong mold and good color, restoration to flat chip under foot ring, unmarked, 14 3/4" by 10". **$1,800-$2,000**

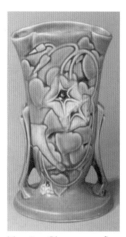

Morning Glory green flaring pillow vase, foil label, 7 1/4" by 4". **$450-$500**

Pair of Morning Glory green candlesticks, minor bruise to base of one, foil label, 5" by 4 1/4". **$450-$500/pair**

Morning Glory green double wall pocket, light glaze scaling (from firing) to tip of shorter holder, unmarked, 8 1/2". **$850-$950**
Right: Morning Glory white pear-shaped vase, 1" tight hairline to rim, grinding chips to base, foil label, 10 1/4" by 7". **$300-$350**
Far right: Morning Glory white flaring vase, small chip to rim, unmarked, 8 1/4" by 6 3/4". **$300-$350**

Morning Glory white oblong planter, strong mold and good color, unmarked, 5" by 13". **$350-$400**

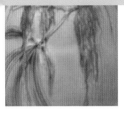

Moss

Another introduction from 1936, Moss evokes the bayou country, with dripping brown glaze hanging from long-leafed branches. Backgrounds include blue, blue-green, tan-brown, and pink-turquoise. Most pieces feature impressed marks.

Moss pink ovoid vase (786-14") with crisp mold and bright color, 1" chip and another restored chip to base, 2" tight line from rim (only goes through at the top), and two small nicks to leaf, impressed mark.

$550-$650

Moss blue wall pocket (278-8"), firing line inside one handle, raised mark.
$400-$450

Moss blue flowerpot (637-5") and under plate, good mold and brilliant color, impressed mark.
$250-$300

Moss blue bulbous vase (783-9"), impressed mark.
$350-$400

Moss blue vase, lines to rim, several small chips to base (some touched up), unmarked, 14 1/2" tall.
$275-$325

Moss green bulbous vase (783-9"), very crisp mold and good color, impressed mark. **$300-$350**

Two Moss urns (779-8" and 776-7"), chip to base and rim of smaller, chips to restored base of larger, both marked.
$375-$425/pair

Moss pink pillow vase (778-7"), impressed mark.
$250-$300

Moss pink console bowl (293-10") with some peppering, impressed mark.
$100-$150

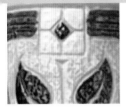

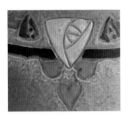

Mostique

Dating from about 1915, Mostique is probably the most common Roseville pattern after Pine Cone, with about 80 different styles known. Crudely stylized leaf and floral patterns, often in spade shapes, alternate with heavy lines and geometric forms on textured bodies of gray or tan. Most pieces are unmarked.

Below left: Two Mostique wall pockets, some scaling and nicks to high points, unmarked, 10".
$350-$400/pair

Below: Mostique jardinière and pedestal, one line and a couple of very minor nicks to jardinière, two small chips and lines to base of pedestal, unmarked; jardinière: 10" tall, pedestal: 18" tall. **$750-$850**

Mostique wall pocket, oval with stylized dogwood (two minor glaze nicks to hole), unmarked, 9 1/2" tall. **$350-$450**

Two Mostique vases, one cylindrical with Glasgow rose (opposing lines, fleck to rim), the other bulbous with papyrus (small flecks), unmarked, 10" and 8" tall.
$325-$375/pair

Mostique pedestal covered in unusual glossy green to amber glaze, restoration to base, chip to top, unmarked, 18" by 11 1/2". **$175-$225**

Three Mostique pieces: two corseted vases and bowl, all decorated with yellow spade-shaped leaves; bowl in as-is condition (chips/cracks), bruise to base of large vase, and glaze chips to all three; each is marked with impressed numbers; vases, 8" tall, 10 1/2" tall, 8 3/4" diameter. **$200-$250/set**

Mostique jardinière with Glasgow roses and spade-shaped leaves in polychrome, a few nicks, unmarked, 9" by 11".
$125-$175

Two Mostique pieces: hanging basket with spade-shaped blossoms (nicks and abrasions) and planter with Glasgow roses; a few glaze flakes overall, "Rv" ink stamp to one; planter: 9" by 10 1/2".   **$275-$325/pair**

Left: Two Mostique vases with spade-shaped flowers, unmarked, 10" and 12".   **$325-$375/pair**

Mostique jardinière with Glasgow roses, some nicks to high points, unmarked, 9 1/2" tall.
$110-$140

Four Mostique pieces: two corseted vases with spade-shaped leaves and two low bowls; hairlines to large bowl, nicks to all, and 1/2" chip to smaller vase, some stamped "Rv"; tallest: 8".   **$225-$275/set**

Normandy

Closely related to Donatello and Corinthian, Normandy (mid-1920s) features a similar color scheme and overall profile, but has a banded tangle of stylized grapevines on a terracotta background. Pieces often have an "Rv" ink stamp.

Normandy hanging basket with good mold and color, "Rv" ink stamp, 7" tall. **$275-$325**

Normandy jardinière, small chip to decoration, "Rv" ink stamp, 10" by 12". **$150 to $200**

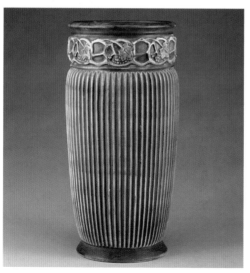

Normandy jardinière with chip and drill-hole to base, unmarked, 8" by 9 1/2". **$125-$175**

Left: Normandy umbrella stand, several small flakes to ribs, bruise and hairlines to base, blue ink stamp, 20" by 10". **$375-$425**

Nursery

Also part of the creamwares, but not to be confused with the Juvenile line, Nursery pieces, circa 1912, have broad rims on low bowls that were suited for feeding in a high chair. They are transfer decorated with about a dozen rhymes, but are otherwise unmarked.

Olympic

Part of the Rozane Wares, Olympic (1905) features transfer images of ancient Greece on a red background and are usually titled. Pieces are sometimes artist signed or marked "Rozane Olympic."

Left: Olympic pitcher, "Ulysses at the Table of Circe," restoration to 5" spider lines from rim, half of the pitcher is overpainted, signed and titled, 7" by 8 1/2".
$1,300-$1,400

Olympic vase, marked on the bottom, "Rozane Olympic Pottery–Minerva, Hector and Mercury" and shape number 56, 12" tall. **$4,000-$5,000**

Right: Rozane Olympic vase, double handled pedestal form, painted mark, "Euryclea discovers Ulysses," 11" tall, minor glaze scratches, restored.
$1,800-$2,200

Courtesy of
Treadway Gallery

Orian

Sometimes misspelled "Orion," this line from 1935 is not a typical art deco motif. The delicate, sinuous handles are more related to art nouveau. The vivid colors include blue, yellow, green, red, peach, and pink with softer accents, and the interiors are frequently a stark contrast: mint with raspberry or turquoise with brown. Pieces can have raised or impressed marks, foil labels, or be unmarked.

Orian classically shaped vase with two buttressed handles, the exterior in glossy raspberry, the interior in mint green, unmarked, 11" by 4".   **$250-$300**

Orian blue double wall pocket, minor flake at hanging point, silver foil label, 8 1/4" by 4".
$750-$850

Orian footed vase with bulbous base and two handles, yellow exterior and blue-green interior, unmarked, 12 1/2" by 4".
$275-$325

Orian peach bowl (272-10") with turquoise interior, impressed mark.
$175-$225

Orian brown vase with squat stepped base, mint green interior, unmarked, 7" by 8".   **$200-$225**

Orian salmon pink vase with squat base and stovepipe neck, unmarked, 6 1/2" by 8 1/2".   **$125-$175**

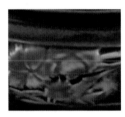

Panel

Part of the Rosecraft line from about 1920, Panel features realistic nudes and floral forms, mostly in one or two colors, on dark brown or green bodies. (This pattern should not be confused with Silhouette from three decades later, which also has nude and floral motifs but in a more stylized form.) Panel is marked with an "Rv" ink stamp.

Panel green wall pocket with nude, short dark crazing line at seam of back and front (most likely in making), "Rv" ink stamp, 7" by 5".   **$500-$600**

Panel flaring buttressed vase with nudes, restoration to several lines from rim, "Rv" ink stamp, 11 1/2" tall. **$400-$500**

Panel brown vase with dandelions, "Rv" ink stamp, 7" by 3 1/4".
$275-$325

Panel brown wall pocket with Baneda pattern, "Rv" ink stamp, 9" by 4 1/4".
$200-$250

Panel green vase with nudes, repaired chips at rim and base, and some shallow scratches, "Rv" ink stamp, 10 1/4" by 5".
$375-$425

Panel green center bowl with purple blossoms, "Rv" ink stamp, 9" diameter.
$150-$200

Panel brown vase with nudes in orange, used as a lamp base but not drilled (includes fittings), several chips to rim; pottery: 10" tall. **$550-$650**

Left: Panel brown flat vase with nudes, two shallow scratches near base, "Rv" ink stamp, 8 1/2" by 6".
$550-$650

Pauleo

This Frederick Rhead design from about 1914 combines the names of Roseville co-founder George Young's daughter-in-law, Pauline, and his daughter, Leota. Commonly found as lamp bases, the simple forms were based on ancient vessels, and the glaze combinations are seemingly limitless. Pieces are frequently unmarked.

Below: Pauleo baluster vase with bulbous body, extremely tapered neck and flaring mouth, in a mottled red and ashen glaze, marked on the bottom with a "Pauleo Pottery" wafer, 10 1/2" tall. **$1,000-$1,200**
Below left: Pauleo classically shaped vase covered in a fine variegated red glaze, several scratches to body and factory drill hole, unmarked, 20 3/4" tall. **$1,100-$1,300**

Pauleo disk vase or bowl in mottled green and pink glazes on a textured background, marked on the bottom with a "Pauleo Pottery" wafer, 7 1/2" by 3".
$1,000-$1,200

Pauleo decorated tall factory lamp base with tulips on a gunmetal ground, in as-is condition (reglued cracks to rim, drilled hole to bottom, nick to body), raised circular mark/231, 16 1/2" by 6 1/2".
$275-$325

Pauleo bulbous vase in smooth orange and brown glaze, a few minor abrasions to rim, unmarked, 18 1/4" tall. **$650-$750**

Pauleo factory lamp base in a pink crackled glaze (rare), unmarked, 19" tall.
$1,300-$1,500

Peony

This line from 1942 features large irregular flower clusters on textured backgrounds that included salmon and green, green and tan, or gold and brown-green, rarely rusty brown. Pieces feature a raised mark, "Roseville U.S.A.," and a style number.

Peony green floor vase (70-18"), minute fleck to one handle and small misfire to one leaf, raised mark. **$350-$400**

Peony green flaring vase (69-15") with strong mold, small chip at rim, raised mark. **$275-$325**

Peony green three-piece tea set: teapot (3), creamer (3-C), and sugar dish (3-S), small chip to base of sugar dish, and minor glaze bubbles to spout of teapot, raised marks. **$225-$275**

Three Peony pieces: pair of green double candlesticks (1153) with some chips to one, and pink cornucopia-shaped vase (170-6"), raised marks. **$90-$110/set**

Two Peony pieces: small pink planter (427-4") and yellow ovoid vase (67-12") with bruise and two restored chips, raised marks. **$125-$175/pair**

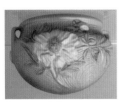

Peony pink hanging basket, several small chips to decoration, marked "U.S.A.," 5 1/2" by 7". **$175-$200**

Above: Two Peony pieces: yellow bulbous vase (63-8") with several chips to flowers and leaves and pink conch shell-shaped piece (436) with fleck to edge of rim and very small bruise to one foot, raised marks. **$125-$175/pair**

Left: Peony pink pedestal, flat chip to rim, several nicks overall, marked "U.S.A." **$90-$110**

Persian

With a strong art nouveau influence, Persian pieces (1908) often feature tight symmetrical designs of stylized scrolls and geometric shapes, with some naturalistic floral motifs, set off by narrow black borders. The line appears to have been limited to jardinières, pedestals, and planters. Pieces are unmarked.

Persian hanging basket with bright coloration, spider lines to base and small chip to one handle, unmarked, 10" tall.
$350-$400

Left: Persian jardinière (462), 5" tall.
Right: Hanging basket, 3 3/4" tall.
$250-$300
$400-$450

Persian planter with stylized pattern in pastel tones, chips to two feet, flecks to rim, unmarked, 4 1/4" by 6 1/2". **$150-$200**

Persian hanging basket, small chip to one hole and two groups of spider lines to body, unmarked, 7 1/2" tall. **$250-$300**

Persian hanging basket, some fading of outlines, opposing 1" hairlines and a bruise to rim, unmarked, 8 1/2" tall. **$200-$225**

Pine Cone

The story of the Pine Cone design is a serendipitous tale of rejection and, ultimately, triumph. The pattern was designed by Frank Ferrel in the early 1900s, but variations were rejected by both Weller and Peters & Reed potteries as unworkable. A sample was also rejected by Roseville, and it languished for years until a Roseville salesman, Charles Snyder, became convinced of its marketability in 1931. The rest is history, and by some estimates, more than 150 styles were created. On backgrounds of blue, orange-brown-tan, or green, it features small ovoid cones with long pine needles on irregular-shaped branches, which may also form the handles of a given piece. In exceedingly rare instances, a pink background may be found. Sometimes unmarked, pieces bear marks that are both raised and impressed, and foil labels are also found. (A late-1940s version with a glossy finish is known as Pine Cone II or Modern.)

Left: Pine Cone blue umbrella stand (777-20") with strong mold and color, raised mark. **$2,400-$2,600**

Pine Cone blue jardinière and pedestal, crisp mold, minor chips and spider lines to base of jardinière, hairline to one handle, pedestal has scaling to pine needle and handle (one touched up), and two repaired chips to rim, both unmarked; jardinière: 12" by 15".
$3,000-$4,000

Pine Cone blue pitcher (1321), good mold, impressed mark, 7 1/2" tall.
$700-$800

Pine Cone blue ewer (851-15"), restoration to hairline on one handle, glaze inconsistency on one side, impressed mark.
$700-$800

Pine Cone blue triple wall pocket (466), raised mark, 4 1/2" by 9". **$1,200-$1,500**

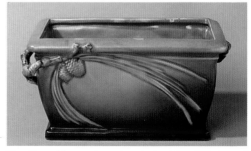

Pine Cone blue urn (912-15"), restoration to rim chip, impressed mark.
$1,700-$1,900

Pine Cone blue rectangular planter (380-10"), several small chips to rim and decoration, impressed mark.
$750-$850

Pine Cone blue flaring pillow vase (492-12"), strong mold and color, raised mark. **$1,400-$1,600**

Pine Cone blue double dish with strong mold, 6 1/2" by 13". **$600-$700**

Three Pine Cone blue tumblers (414-5"), raised mark. **$800-$900/set**

Pine Cone blue ewer (909-10"), impressed mark, and remnant of gold foil label. **$550-$650**

Two Pine Cone blue smoking pieces: small leaf-shaped ashtray (499) and cigarette holder (498), raised marks; 4 3/4" diameter and 2 3/4" tall. **$450-$550/pair**

Pair of Pine Cone blue cups (960-4"), raised marks. **$500-$600/pair**

Pine Cone blue basket (410-10"), raised mark. **$400-$500**

Pine Cone blue vase, flaring, foil label on body, 11 1/2" by 6". **$600-$700**

Pine Cone blue urn, restoration to base, unmarked, 14 1/4" by 8 1/2". **$600-$700**

Pine Cone blue triple bud vase, unmarked, 8 1/2". **$400-$500**

Pine Cone blue corseted vase with squat base (712-12"), very strong mold and color, raised mark. **$700-$800**

Right: Pine Cone blue fan vase (472-6"), overall peppering, raised mark. **$375-$425**

Pine Cone blue flaring vase with basket handle (936-10"), marked. **$400-$450**

Pine Cone blue spherical vase (746-7"), several small chips to base, some scratches, impressed mark. **$275-$325**

Pine Cone blue bowl (321-9"), impressed mark. **$300-$350**

Pair of Pine Cone brown bookend planters (459), minor firing chip to bottom ring of one, raised mark, 5 1/4" by 5" by 5".
$800-$1,000/pair

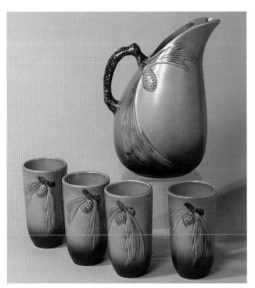

Pine Cone brown cider set with pitcher (415-9") and four tumblers (414-5"), raised marks. **$1,400-$1,500/set**

Pine Cone brown basket (339), restoration to chip at base, impressed mark, 11" by 13 1/4" by 9 3/4".
$550-$650

Four Pine Cone brown candlesticks: two triple (1106-5 1/2") and two single (1123), hairlines to two, raised marks. **$550-$650/set**

Pine Cone brown hanging basket, short and shallow horizontal line to rim, and a few minute flecks to body and hanging holes, marked "U.S.A.," 5 1/2" tall. **$125-$175**

Left: Pine Cone brown center bowl (322-12"), impressed mark. **$225-$275**

Pine Cone brown jardinière and pedestal with strong mold, extensive restoration to both jardinière and pedestal, unmarked; jardinière: 11" tall, pedestal: 18" tall.

$600-$700

Pine Cone brown spherical jardinière (632-7"), impressed mark.

$400-$450

Right: Five brown Pine Cone pieces: mint spherical pitcher (1321) with ice lip, and four cups (960-4), three of which are in as-is condition (chips, crack), impressed mark; pitcher: 8" by 8 3/4". **$550-$650**

Three Pine Cone brown pieces: tall footed vase, vase with squat base (842-8"), and small jardinière (632-3"), impressed marks on two; tall vase: 9 3/4".

$750-$850/group

Pine Cone brown bulbous pitcher, several minor nicks to pine cones, unmarked, 9 1/2" by 8 1/2".

$450-$550

Pine Cone brown flowerpot (633-5"), missing under plate, very tight short line to interior rim, raised mark, 5 1/4" by 6 1/2".

$110-$140

Pine Cone brown urn (844-8") with crisp mold, glaze flake inside both handles (possibly in manufacture), raised mark.
$350-$400

Pine Cone brown urn (848-10") with very crisp mold, raised mark.
$450-$550

Pine Cone brown floor vase (913-18") with good mold and color, repair to rim and base, incised mark.
$700-$900

Pine Cone brown four-sided pillow vase (114-8"), soft mold, small nick to one pine cone, impressed mark.
$350-$450

Two Pine Cone Modern pieces:
Basket (408-6"), raised mark **$350-$450**
Candleholder (451-4"), raised mark. **$350-$400**

Pine Cone Modern planter (472-8"), raised mark.
$400-$500

Pine Cone Modern double serving tray (462), unmarked, 6" by 13 1/4".
$350-$450

Pine Cone green basket (409-8"), raised mark.
$300-$350

Below: Pine Cone green canoe-shaped planter (431-15"), 1/2" flat chip to base ring, raised mark.
$125-$175

Pine Cone green ewer (851-15"), impressed mark. **$700-$800**

Pine Cone green bulbous vase (856-12"), impressed mark. **$450-$550**

Pine Cone green ewer (416-18"), restored chip to spout, and minor firing flaw to base, raised mark.
$400-$450

Two Pine Cone green pieces: rare cylindrical vase with flaring rim (short tight line to one leaf), and triple bud vase, unmarked, 8 1/4" tall each. **$300-$350/pair**

Pine Cone green handled bowl (410-10"), several repairs to cracks on handle, raised mark. **$125-$175**

Pine Cone green flaring vase (492-12"), restoration to rim and dividing bar, marked. **$300-$350**

Two Pine Cone green pieces: rectangular dish (430-12") with strong mold and gravy boat (455-6") with chip to handle, raised marks. **$225-$275/pair**

Pine Cone green jardinière (632-8") with strong mold, chips to base and line from rim, foil label. **$325-$375**

Pine Cone green center bowl, short tight line from rim and minor grinding chips, unmarked, 4 1/4" by 11". **$110-$140**

Pine Cone green footed planter with scalloped rim (458F-5"), glaze scaling to handles, impressed mark. **$150-$200**

Poppy

Introduced in 1938, Poppy features flowers, both in full bloom and in buds, on slender waving stems. Backgrounds may be yellow-brown, pale yellow and dusty blue, green and orange-pink, salmon and yellow, or pink, yellow, and brown. Marks are often impressed, rarely raised, and sometimes pieces are unmarked.

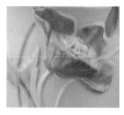

Poppy green jardinière and pedestal set, 1/4" chip and clay pimple to base of jardinière, unmarked; jardinière: 10" tall, pedestal: 16" tall. **$700-$800**

Poppy pink ewer (880-18"), good mold, minor peppering to spout, impressed mark.**$550-$650**

Poppy green bulbous vase (875-10") with repair and bruise to base, and nick to flower, impressed mark. **$150-$200**

Poppy brown vessel on squat base (873-9"), restoration around base, impressed mark, rare. **$450-$550**

Poppy green basket (347-10"), raised mark. **$250-$300**

Poppy pink urn (869-7"), short firing line to base, impressed mark. **$125-$175**

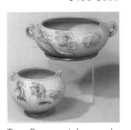

Two Poppy pink vessels: small jardinière (642-3") and low bowl (336-5"), short tight line to rim of jardinière, impressed marks, silver foil label on one. **$110-$140/pair**

Poppy green ovoid floor vase (829-18"), impressed mark. **$600-$700**

Poppy squat vessel with handles, unmarked, 4" by 7 5/8" by 5 7/8". **$250-$350**

Right: Poppy pink ewer (876-10"), good mold, impressed mark. **$250-$300**

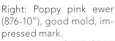

Poppy gray-blue planter and double candleholder (341-7"), impressed mark, 8" by 8 1/2". **$225-$275**

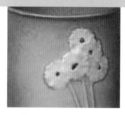

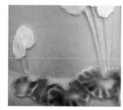

Primrose

From 1936, Primrose features tiny white blossoms on spindly stems emerging from a cluster of green leaves. Backgrounds are blue, brown-yellow-tan, or salmon pink. Pieces have impressed marks.

Primrose blue ovoid vase (770-10"), impressed mark. **$300-$350**

Primrose blue vase (772-14"), two minor flakes to base, impressed mark. **$400-$450**

Primrose blue jardinière (634-8") and pedestal, jardinière has 6" line to body (goes through to interior) and several quarter-size patches of glaze scaling; pedestal has restoration to crack around base, impressed mark. **$375-$425**

Primrose blue bulbous jardinière (634-7"), nick with several lines to one handle, impressed mark. **$90-$110**

Primrose pink wall pocket (1277-8"), impressed mark. **$550-$600**

Three Primrose pink candlesticks, one triple (1113) and a pair (1105-4 1/2"), impressed marks; triple: 5 1/2" by 5 1/2" **$275-$325/set**

Two Primrose brown vases, one bulbous (767-8") with touch-up to corner of one handle and to small rim chip, and one shouldered (760-6"), impressed marks. **$175-$225/pair**

Two Primrose pink pieces: vase (762-7") and cornucopia (125) with small rim chip, impressed marks; cornucopia: 6 1/2" by 5". **$175-$200/pair**

Two Primrose brown pieces: squat jardinière with soft mold (284-4") and vase (763-7") with restoration to 1/2" rim chip, impressed marks. **$200-$250/pair**

Primrose pink urn (764-7"), marked. **$70-$90**

Left: Primrose brown bulbous jardinière (634-5"), impressed mark. **$250-$300**

Q

Quaker

Quaker

From the first quarter of the 20th century, these creamware pieces have a band of jolly Quakers smoking pipes around the tops of the vessels. All are unmarked.

Quaker cup or jar (may have had lid), unmarked, cracks, 4 3/8" by 3 1/2".　　$90-$120

Raymor

Almost the last gasp for Roseville, Raymor—designed by Ben Siebel and introduced in 1953—did not meet with the success that the company had hoped for. This line of sleek, elliptical forms with a high gloss includes Modern Artware and Modern Stoneware, and a Gourmet group from 1954. Pieces feature raised or impressed marks. Now being embraced by collectors of modernist designs, this pattern still represents a good value for beginners.

Left: Raymor/Modern Artware lantern wall pocket covered in a glossy chartreuse glaze, three small chips to one edge, impressed 711, and paper labels, 10" tall.
$300-$350
Below: Two Raymor bowls: a brown "Lug Fruit," (192), and a covered baking dish in ivory, indistinct style number.
$50-$60/pair

Rosecraft Color

From 1916, the Color line of Rosecraft has more than 60 shapes in solid colors of blue, green, red, and yellow. Pieces are often unmarked or have an "Rv" stamp.

Rosecraft Color pink hanging basket with three loop handles, unmarked, 4" by 7".
$75-$100

Rosecraft Vintage

The Rosecraft Vintage line from 1924 was also strongly influenced by art nouveau design, with stylized grapevines ringing classically shaped vessels of dark brown. Pieces often feature an "Rv" ink stamp.

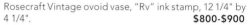

Rosecraft Vintage ovoid vase, "Rv" ink stamp, 12 1/4" by 4 1/4". **$800-$900**

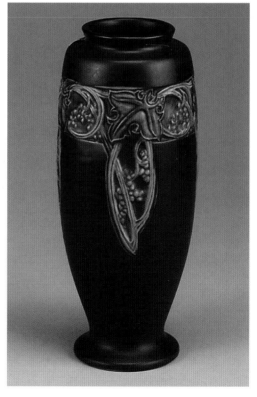

Rosecraft Vintage wall pocket, "Rv" ink stamp, 9" tall. **$375-$425**

Rosecraft Vintage rectangular planter complete with liner, "Rv" ink stamp, 5 1/2" by 11". **$800-$900**

Rosecraft Vintage jardiniere with very strong mold, no visible mark, 9 1/4" by 12". **$375-$425**

Rosecraft Vintage bulbous vase, "Rv" ink stamp, 10 1/2" by 7". **$550-$650**

Rosecraft Vintage classically shaped vase with strong mold, "Rv" ink stamp, 8 1/2" by 6". **$500-$550**

Rosecraft Vintage double bud vase, nick to base, "Rv" ink stamp, 5" by 7 1/2". **$400-$450**

Two Rosecraft Vintage vases: barrel-shaped vase (painted over glaze flaking) and bulbous (kiln "kiss" to body), "Rv" ink stamp, each 6 1/4" tall. **$325-$375/pair**

Rosecraft Vintage squat vessel, "Rv" ink stamp, 3" by 4 1/2". **$200-$250**

Rosecraft Vintage bowl with crisp mold, "Rv" ink stamp, 2" by 7 1/2". **$225-$275**

Royal Capri

Another line that failed to meet expectations, Royal Capri, with its mottled glossy and matt gold finish, was produced near the end Roseville Pottery's existence. Pieces are hard to find in mint condition. They feature raised marks.

Royal Capri scalloped bowl (526-7"), minor wear to gold at rim, raised mark. **$175-$200**

Four pieces of Royal Capri:
Vase (579-8") is 8 1/2" tall **$225-$275**
Scalloped bowl (527-7") on right is 7 1/2 in diameter **$200-$225**
Console bowl (526-7") center is 7 1/2" diameter **$200-$225**
Small footed pot (faint mark) foreground is 2 3/4" tall. **$200-$225**

Rozane Line, 1917

Often identified as Rozane Line or Rozane 1917, these wares are at the opposite end of the design spectrum from Rozane Royal. It has heavy floral and leaf patterns on a textured body, usually cream or pale green. Pieces are usually unmarked and rarely stamped.

Left: Rozane 1917 jardinière, unmarked, 8 1/2" by 9".
$125-$175
Below: Two Rozane 1917 pieces: green jardinière (bruise to rim and repairs to flowers) and ivory vase, Rozane stamp mark to one; jardinière: 9" tall. **$150-$200/pair**

Left: Two Rozane 1917 pieces: center bowl and handled vase; line to rim and some small chips to decoration on bowl; repaired handles to vase, one marked; bowl: 7 1/2" diameter; vase: 5 1/4" tall. **$110-$140/pair**

Rozane Pattern

This line from 1941 bears the Rozane name, but the similarities to earlier Rozane lines end there. These shapes are mostly sleek and modern, with bright solid colors of blue, green, and terra cotta, and a few in mottled matte glazes that blend pastel shades. Pieces have raised marks.

Rozane Pattern footed vase with flaring rim (11-15"), covered in a mottled blue-green matte glaze, raised mark. **$450-$500**

Two Rozane Pattern pieces: vase (7-9") and urn (5-8") with minor bruise to rim, both covered in a mottled blue-green matte glaze, raised marks. **$300-$350/pair**

Two Rozane Pattern vases with buttressed base, (9-10") with several chips to inner foot ring, and (10-12"), both covered in a glossy vermillion glaze, raised marks. **$250-$275/pair**

Left: Six Rozane Pattern pieces, 1940s, four in glossy blue: low bowl (396-10"), vase (2-6"), large footed cornucopia (2), and feather ornament (2) with broken tip; and two in glossy terra cotta: two-handled vase (1-6") and fish ornament (1), raised marks; cornucopia: 5" by 12". **$350-$400/set**

Rozane/ Rozane Royal

Designed to compete with similar lines by Weller and Rookwood, Rozane (which combined the names Roseville and Zanesville) was introduced shortly after the turn of the 19th century, and the artists who created these pieces were left to their own stylistic devices. Many pieces have floral motifs, others featured portraits, some hunting dogs, still others had harvest themes or birds. Though most backgrounds are a glossy black-brown, others are called Royal Light and have ivory or pastel tones. Pieces are often artist signed or stamped "Rozane RPCo." or "Rozane Royal Ware" on a wafer/seal.

Rozane Royal Light vase painted by Mae Timberlake with yellow daffodils, small bruise to rim, signed "Mae Timberlake" with Rozane wafer, 10 3/4" tall. **$500-$600**

Rozane Royal Dark pillow vase, shape No. 882, hand-painted with a hunting dog with a pheasant in its mouth, signed "Timberlake," marked with raised stamp, "Rozane Royal Ware," 10 3/4" by 9" by 6 1/4". **$3,500-$4,500**

Rozane Royal Dark tall vase painted with yellow and brown daisies, a few minor flecks to body and rim, stamped "ROZANE 837 RPCO."; 13" by 7". **$225-$275**

Rozane Royal Light vase painted with flowers, Rozane Royal wafer, 10 1/2" tall. **$350-$450**

Rozane jardinière and pedestal painted by W. Myers with yellow tea roses, flakes and scratches to both pieces, chips to foot of pedestal, artist-signed on pedestal, 32" tall overall. **$900-$1,100**

Rozane Royal Dark tear-shaped vase, painted by H. Dunlavy with a Turkish man in profile, hairline from rim, Rozane wafer and artist's signature, 8" by 5". **$1,100-$1,300**

Rozane Royal Dark bulbous vase, painted with poppies (?), stamped "ROZANE 806 RPCO."; 8" by 4 1/2". **$750-$850**

Rozane Royal Light spherical jardinière on three feet, painted with lavender, white, and gray tulips, fine overall crazing, touched-up nick to inner rim, a couple of pock marks, and glaze flakes to feet, unmarked, 10" by 13". **$110-$140**

Rozane Royal Dark pitcher painted with cherries, illegible artist's initials, marked "ROZANE 890 RPCO," 12 1/4" by 6 1/2". **$600-$700**

Rozane pitcher painted with Lily of the Valley, nick and repaired chips to base, Rozane Ware seal, 7 1/2" tall. **$110-$140**

Rozane Royal Dark bottle-shaped vase painted with brown carnations, stamped "ROZANE/ RPCO/919," 8" by 4 1/2". **$175-$225**

Rozane Royal Dark ovoid vase painted with a yellow crocus, pockmarks and scratches, impressed mark, 6 1/2" by 3 3/4". **$150-$200**

Rozane Royal Dark bud vase painted with palm fronds on a black to green ground, small bruises to rim, stamped "Rozane RPCO/ W.H.," 8" tall. **$125-$175**

Rozane Royal Dark pitcher painted by W. Meyers with branches of cherries, lifting of overglaze (some touch-up), Rozane wafer, 15 3/4" tall. **$200-$250**

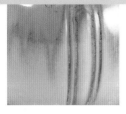

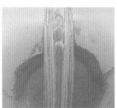

Russco

Introduced in 1934, the Russco shapes have a strong art deco influence, but the glazes are often freeform, either blended or crystalline, green and beige or tan and brown being the most common. Some have interiors with iridescent surfaces. Pieces are unmarked or have paper labels.

Russco bulbous vase with flaring rim in amber and gold crystalline glazes, unmarked, 10" by 6 1/2".
$350-$450

Russco faceted flaring bowl, exterior in gold crystalline, interior in green and brown, unmarked, 4" by 8".
$150-$175

Russco vase in gold and green crystalline glazes, repair and nicks to 3" section of base, unmarked, 6 1/2" by 6 1/2". **$250-$300**

Russco orange-yellow footed vase, some tiny nicks to rim and base, unmarked, 7 1/2" by 7 1/2".
$125-$175

Russco urn in green and beige crystalline glazes, minute fleck to rim and restoration to small chip at base, unmarked, 8 1/4" by 6". **$70-$90**

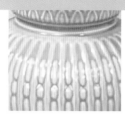

Savona

The fluted, bulbous profile of Savona (mid-1920s) is accented by evenly spaced floral garlands on some pieces. Bright glossy solid colors include green and yellow, plus the subtler dusty blue, salmon, and ivory. Pieces are unmarked or have foil/paper labels.

Left: Savona yellow covered vessel, black paper label, 4" by 8".
$800-$900

Savona green four-sided vase with touch-ups to two shallow chips on bottom ring (not visible on side), unmarked, 10 1/2" by 3". **$325-$350**

Pair of Savona urns, one apricot and one blue, peppering and restoration to a couple of areas at base, and opposing lines to rim of apricot urn, unmarked, 12" by 7" each. **$300-$400/pair**

Savona green classically shaped vase with burst bubbles around rim and base, unmarked, 12" by 6 1/2". **$250-$300**

Savona classically shaped vase in blue-gray, unmarked, 12" by 5 1/2". **$200-$250**

Savona yellow classically shaped vase, unmarked, 12 1/4" by 6". **$250-$300**

Savona blue console set, black paper label on bowl; candlesticks: 4" by 4"; bowl: 4" by 10". **$275-$325/set**

Savona ivory console set, hairline to one handle on each candlestick, 4" line to bowl (does not go through), silver foil label on bowl; candlesticks: 4" by 4"; bowl: 2 1/2" by 10 1/2". **$200-$225/set**

Far left: Savona blue wall pocket, unmarked, 8 1/4" tall. **$450-$550**
Left: Savona apricot bulbous vase, 1/2" bruise to one handle, unmarked, 6" by 5 1/2". **$150-$200**

Silhouette

This line from 1950 is a mix of stylistic influences, sleek and chunky, bulbous and angular. With panels of female nudes or floral motifs on dark backgrounds, the bodies are muted solid colors, usually of blue-green, raspberry, brown, and white. Pieces feature raised marks or are stamped "U.S.A."

Four Silhouette pieces: red double planter (757-9") with nick to base, two ovoid planters (779-5") in red and white with oak leaves, and small white pitcher (716-6") with acorns, all marked. **$225-$275/set**

Silhouette pink vase (783-7") with female nude in profile, raised mark, 7 7/8" by 7 3/8" by 3 3/4". **$650-$750**

Silhouette brown bulbous vase (742-6") with 1" bruise to base, raised mark. **$425-$475**

Silhouette brown hanging basket embossed with ivy, stamped "U.S.A.," 4 1/4" by 5 1/2". **$150-$175**

Silhouette pink wall pocket (766-8") with ivy leaves, raised mark. **$250-$300**

Three Silhouette pieces: one green and one white with branch of leaves, and one brown with oak leaf (repair to one corner), all marked. **$125-$175/set**

Silhouette blue basket (710-10") with panels of tropical blossoms, raised mark. **$70-$90**

Above left: Silhouette covered box with blooming branch (740), some flat chips to lid and to base, raised mark, 2 3/4" by 4 1/4". **$35-$45**
Above right: Silhouette brown lidded box (740) with branch and blossom, raised mark, 3" by 4 1/2". **$175-$225**

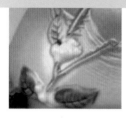

Snowberry

Gardeners may know the plant on this line of pottery as "symphoricarpos," while others will quickly recognize the clumps of white berries that give it its name. Introduced in 1947, this pattern also has a special letter code to identify shapes. Colors are a blend of variegated green and tan, pink-tan to burgundy, and blue to mauve. Most pieces have raised marks.

Snowberry green jardinière (IJ-8) and pedestal (IP-8), bruise to top of pedestal, both marked. **$550-$650**

Snowberry pink floor vase (IV-18"), glazed over or touched-up nick to one handle, raised mark.
$375-$425

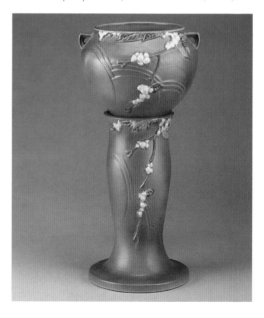

Snowberry blue three-piece tea set, nicks to spout of teapot, cracks to creamer (1C), all marked. **$225-$275/set**

Three Snowberry blue pieces: pair of ewers (ITK-6") and console bowl (IBL2-12) with small chips to rim and nick to handle, raised marks. **$250-$300/set**

Pair of Snowberry blue cornucopia vases (1CC-6"), minor flat chip to base, fleck to rim of one (shows slightly on side), small fleck to base of the other, raised marks. **$100-$125/pair**

Two Snowberry pieces: blue chalice vase (IUR-8") and pink ashtray (colored-in stilt pull chips), both marked; ashtray: 5 1/4" diameter. **$110-$140/pair**

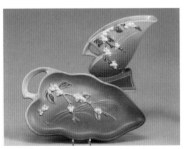

Three Snowberry green pieces: rectangular planter (IWX), round dish (IBLI-6") with small chip to rim and bruise to berry, and hanging basket with opposing cracks; two marked; hanging basket: 6" tall. **$225-$275/set**

Two Snowberry pieces: blue leaf-shaped tray (1BL1-12) and pillow vessel (1FH-7") with small chip to rim, both marked. **$100-$150/pair**

Two Snowberry pieces: green urn (IUR-8") with short line to base (most likely in making) and pink wall pocket (IWP-8"), both marked.   **$225-$275/pair**

Six Snowberry pieces: pair of low pink candlesticks (ICS1), tall pink candlestick (ICS2) with small filled-in chip, pink bowl (IBL-8") with chip to rim, green jardinière (IJ-4), and pink jardinière (IJ-6"), all marked.   **$300-$350/set**

Snowberry green candlesticks (1CS1), raised mark.   **$225-$275**

Four Snowberry pieces: pink ewer (ITK10) with chips to base, small pink dish, pink vase (IVI-7") with fleck to base and glaze chip to rim, and green vase (IV-6"), all marked.   **$250-$300/set**

Two Snowberry pieces: green basket (IBK-10") and pink cornucopia vase (1CC-8"), raised marks.   **$275-$325**

Five Snowberry pieces: pink cornucopia vase with glaze scaling, possibly in making; two green bowls with chip to one; green vase; and blue leaf-shaped tray with small chip, all marked. **$225-$275/set**

Three Snowberry pieces: pair of pink bud vases (IBV-7") with small chips to base of one and green hanging basket (chip to one handle and line from rim), vases marked; basket: 8" diameter. **$125-$175/set**

Pair of Snowberry pink hanging baskets, some minor nicks and minor abrasion to one hanging hole, unmarked, 5" tall each. **$175-$225/pair**

Snowberry green basket (1BK-8"), raised mark. **$250-$300**

Snowberry pink tea set (1) with clay burst to handle of creamer (in the firing), raised marks; teapot: 7 1/4" by 10 1/2". **$250-$300/set**

Snowberry pink cornucopia vase (1CC-6"), raised mark, 6" by 4" by 5 1/4". **$100-$140**

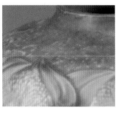

Sunflower

Introduced in 1930 and now one of the most popular Roseville lines, these pieces are ringed with large yellow blossoms on bending stems that march in lock step at regular intervals. In descending order on the rough textured surface are brown, green, and blue, mottled with ivory or yellow. Pieces are unmarked or with black paper labels.

Sunflower jardinière and pedestal with excellent mold and color, restoration to chip at rim of jardinière, a few small flecks, unmarked; jardinière: 10 1/2" tall; pedestal: 18 1/2" tall.   **$4,200-$4,300**

Pair of Sunflower candlesticks, soft mold, one has hairline to stem, black paper label on both, 4 1/4" by 3 3/4" each.
$500-$600/pair

Sunflower bulbous vase with collared rim, soft mold, unmarked, 9 1/4" by 6 3/4". **$1,200-$1,400**

Sunflower bulbous vase, excellent mold and color, unmarked, 8 1/4" by 6 1/2". **$1,100-$1,300**

Sunflower bulbous vase with strong mold and good color, tight 1" bruise to rim, unmarked, 9 1/2" tall. **$1,400-$1,600**

Sunflower jardinière with very strong mold and color, two tiny repairs at rim, two flecks to the leaves on body, unmarked, 13" by 16". **$2,200-$2,400**

Sunflower ovoid vase, excellent mold and color, unmarked, 10 1/4" by 6 1/4". **$2,000-$2,200**

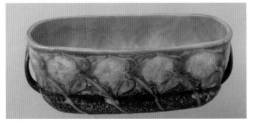

Left: Sunflower four-sided planter, unmarked, rare, 3 3/4" by 11".
$1,000-$1,200

Sunflower flaring vase, good mold, unmarked, 7 1/4" by 5". **$900-$1,000**

Sunflower spherical vase, remnant of black paper label, 6 1/4" by 7 1/2".
$800-$900

Two Sunflower two-handled vases, soft mold to both, one has restoration to body chip and rim chip, unmarked, 5 1/4" by 4 1/4" and 6" by 5". **$650-$750/pair**

Sunflower shouldered low bowl, burst bubble to one leaf, unmarked, 4" by 7 1/4". **$400-$475**

Sunflower hanging basket, 1 1/2" spider line from rim, unmarked, 5" by 7". **$450-$550**

Sunflower two-handled vase, unmarked, 5" tall.
$375-$425

Left: Sunflower bulbous vase with good color, small burst to decoration and nick to foot ring (does not show on side), unmarked, 5 1/4" by 5".
$450-$550

Sylvan

A rustic pattern from the first quarter of the 20th century, Sylvan pieces featured textured surfaces in colors of brown, tan, and muddy green, with leafy decoration, and some animal motifs, including hunting dogs, a fox and chickens, birds, and squirrels. Interiors are usually a glossy green. All are unmarked.

Left:Sylvan chalice vase decorated with fox and chickens, with olive-green glossy glazed interior, unmarked, 9 1/2" by 4".   **$600-$700**
Below right: Sylvan umbrella stand (750-21") with olive-green glossy glazed interior, unmarked, with rim chip, 21 1/2" by 10".   **$700-$800**

Above: Sylvan jardinière decorated with hunting dogs, with olive-green glossy glazed interior, unmarked, 10" by 12 1/2".   **$1,500-$1,600**

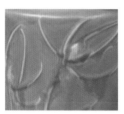

Teasel

The stylized plant form on Teasel (1938) is usually covered in dripping or blended glazes of dusty blue or pink, ivory, brown, and even sea foam green, sometimes set off by metallic accents. Pieces usually have impressed marks.

Teasel sea foam bulbous vase (889-15"), impressed mark. **$500-$600**

Teasel blue ewer (890-18"), impressed mark. **$500-$600**

Teasel pink spherical vessel (343-6") with small nick to one flower, impressed mark. **$150-$175**

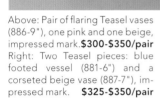

Above: Pair of flaring Teasel vases (886-9"), one pink and one beige, impressed mark.**$300-$350/pair**
Right: Two Teasel pieces: blue footed vessel (881-6") and a corseted beige vase (887-7"), impressed mark. **$325-$350/pair**

Teasel blue bulbous vase (884-8"), impressed mark. **$175-$200**

Teasel beige basket (349-10"), unmarked. **$250-$275**

Teasel blue flaring urn (888-12"), impressed mark. **$375-$425**

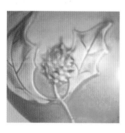

Thorn Apple

Introduced in 1937, Thorn Apple has a tapering blossom on one side of the vessel and a thorny pod on the other. Background colors are blue fading to turquoise, brown to tan with yellow accents, and green with a salmon pink. Pieces usually have impressed marks.

Two Thorn Apple brown pieces: wall pocket (1280-8") with clay pimple to body and vase (810-6") with minute fleck to handle, impressed marks. **$400-$450/pair**

Thorn Apple pink wall pocket, unmarked, 9 1/4" tall. **$450-$550**

Two Thorn Apple pieces: brown pillow vase (812-6") and pink bowl (307-6"), both marked. **$250-$300/pair**

Thorn Apple pink pedestal, unmarked, 17".
$275-$325

Three Thorn Apple brown pieces: triple candleholder (1120) and pair of cornucopia-shaped vases (127-6"), a couple of tiny flecks to one, impressed marks.
$200-$250/set

Thorn Apple candlesticks obscured marked, 2 1/2" tall.
$150-$200/pair

Thorn Apple brown hanging basket, tight 1" line to one hole, unmarked, 5 3/4" by 7 1/2".
$225-$275

Two Thorn Apple pieces: pink squat vase (808-4") with bruise to rim and blue bulbous vase (818-8"), impressed marks.
$200-$250/pair

Thorn Apple blue vase, small chip to base, marked, 10" tall.
$150-$200

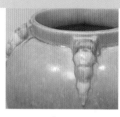

Topeo

A generally bulbous line from 1934, Topeo has symmetrical tapering garlands that look like small cabbages in certain glaze combinations. Often found in blue-green turquoise, there is also a blood red. Pieces are unmarked or have a foil label.

Topeo blue console set, silver foil label on bowl; bowl: 4 1/4" by 12 3/4", candlesticks: 4" tall. **$500-$600**

Topeo blue bulbous vessel, unmarked, 9 1/2" by 5 1/2". **$450-$550**

Topeo red low bowl, unmarked, 2 3/4" by 8 1/4". **$90-$110**

Topeo blue tapering vase, unmarked, 8 1/2" tall.
$450-$550

Two Topeo blue pieces: squat center bowl and ovoid vase; short tight line to rim of vase, unmarked; 11" diameter and 6 3/4" by 4".
$300-$350/pair

Topeo blue spherical vessel, unmarked, 6 1/4" by 7".
$350-$400

Topeo red ovoid vase with very strong mold, unmarked, 9 1/4" by 6 3/4".
$300-$350

Topeo red (sometimes called "Mowa") bulbous vase and Artcraft red planter; some scratches and flecks to both, 1" crack to base of planter, foil label to one, 7" and 4" tall.
$90-$110/pair

Tourist

Part of the creamwares, Tourist pieces date to about 1910 and feature a wide banded motif showing touring cars on a day in the country. Pieces are unmarked.

Tourist jardinière, unmarked, 7 1/4" by 8 1/2".
$2,200-$2,400

Tourist planter or window box, minor paint flaking, 6 7/8" by 7 7/8" by 13". **$2,500-$3,000**

Tourist pedestal, 3/4" tight line to rim (in making?) and very minor losses to paint, unmarked, 21 1/2" tall by 11" diameter at base. **$2,100-$2,300**

Above: Tourist trumpet vase, unmarked, 7 3/4" by 5". **$1,500-$1,700**
Right: Tourist bowl, 3" by 5 1/2". **$2,400-$2,500**

Courtesy Adamstown Antique Gallery

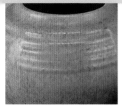

Tourmaline

Introduced in 1933, Tourmaline has a distinctive ribbed band on many of its pieces and a mottled dripping glaze combination that includes blue, ivory, tan, turquoise, raspberry, and amber-yellow. Pieces are unmarked or have a foil label.

Two Tourmaline pieces: bulbous vase (line and large repaired chip to rim) and a cornucopia-shaped vase (several very minor grinding chips), both unmarked; taller: 7 1/2". **$125-$150/pair**

Tourmaline ovoid vase, unmarked, 7 1/2" by 3 1/2". **$250-$300**

Left: Two Tourmaline pieces: shouldered jardinière and tall faceted vase embossed with circles, covered in a mottled blue-green glaze, one has foil label, 5" and 10 1/4" tall.
$450-$500/pair

Two spherical vases: Tourmaline and turquoise Matt Color, foil labels, 5 1/4" and 3 1/4" tall.**$350-$450/pair**

Tourmaline blue two-handled bulbous vase, minor grinding chips and abrasions, foil label, 5 3/4" by 6 1/4".   **$110-$140**

Above: Two Tourmaline blue bulbous vessels, one has 2 1/2" crack from rim, unmarked, 7 1/2" by 6 1/4" each.   **$250-$300/pair**
Two Tourmaline vases: twisted faceted (restoration to rim chip) and flaring (small chip to top), both covered in a mottled pink and blue matte glaze, unmarked, both 8 1/4" tall. **$150-$175/pair**

Tuscany

From the mid-1920s, Tuscany has a mottled glaze on classically shaped vessels, and handles in the shape of grape clusters and leaves. Pink is more common than gray. Pieces are unmarked or have a paper label.

Two Tuscany pink pieces: footed bowl (some short tight lines to rim) and bulbous vase (restorations to rim and base), unmarked, 9 3/4" diameter and 8 3/4" by 7". **$100-$150/pair**

Tuscany footed bowl, black label, 6 1/4" by 4 1/8". **$150-$170**

Tuscany pink squat vessel, spider lines to base, unmarked, 5 1/2" by 7". **$75-$85**

Two Tuscany wall pockets: one gray and one pink, chip to hole on both, unmarked, 8 1/2" and 7 1/2" tall. **$225-$250/pair**

Tuscany pink candleholder, unmarked, 3 7/8" by 3 7/8". **$50-$70**

Utility Ware

Made over two decades until the 1940s, these simple bowls and pitchers had a wide band of solid color accented by black or gray pinstripes. A few examples have hand-painted flowers or landscapes, and others have stylized leaves. Pieces feature the "Rv" ink stamp.

Decorated Utility Ware pitcher with blue stripe, "Rv" ink stamp, 8" tall. **$175-$200**

Four decorated Utility Ware pitchers, a few nicks and scratches overall, dark crazing to one, "Rv" ink stamps; tallest: 7 1/2". **$225-$275/set**

Decorated Utility Ware mixing bowl with green stripe, "Rv" ink stamp, 9" diameter. **$125-$150**

Four decorated Utility Ware pieces: three bowls and pitcher painted with stripes; small chip to pitcher and some hairlines to smallest bowl, "Rv" ink stamps; largest: 6" by 9 1/2" **$200-$250/set**

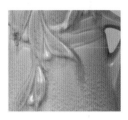

Velmoss

The Velmoss name is associated with three distinct Roseville lines, two of which are described here. The early Velmoss has an Arts & Crafts aura and is a dull green or tan blend with large stylized vertical leaves cloaking the vessels. Pieces are unmarked.

Velmoss II (1935) has naturalistic leaves draped over a wavy ridged border with background colors of muted greens, blues, and pinks. Pieces occasionally feature impressed marks, but are mostly unmarked or have a foil label.

Left: Velmoss early cylindrical vase, glaze fleck to one leaf, unmarked, 9" tall.   **$500-$600**
Below: Velmoss early jardinière, some minor flakes, unmarked, 12" by 16".   **$1,350-$1,450**

Early Velmoss bulbous vase with flared mouth (129-8"), 8" tall. **$900-$1,000**

Early Velmoss jardinière, unmarked, 7" tall.
$800-$900

Early Velmoss tapering vase (136-10"), unmarked, 10" tall. **$900-$1,000**

Velmoss II pink vase, gold foil label, 14 1/4" by 8 3/4". **$600-$700**

Left: Two Velmoss II vases, one blue and one pink, unmarked, 6 1/4" by 5 3/4" and 7 1/4" by 5 1/2". **$400-$500/ pair**

Velmoss II bulbous vase, 1/2" touch-up to rim, unmarked, 12 1/4" by 6 1/4". **$150-$175**

Two Velmoss II double bud vases, one green and one blue, blue has silver foil label, 8 1/4" by 5" and 8 3/4" by 7 1/4". **$250-$350/pair**

Velmoss Scroll

Dating from just before 1920, and once known as Velmoss I, this highly stylized design has a pattern of roses, leaves, and stems on a cream body. Pieces are unmarked.

Right: Velmoss Scroll console set consisting of flaring footed bowl (strong mold, restored chip to rim) and pair of tall candlesticks, unmarked; bowl: 5" by 9", sticks: 8 1/4" tall. **$250-$300/set**

Two Velmoss Scroll vases: one corseted (1/4" chip to base) and one cylindrical bud, unmarked, 10" and 6 1/4" tall. **$275-$325/pair**

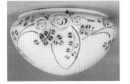

Left: Velmoss Scroll hanging basket with 3" line from rim and 2" line to bottom, unmarked, 7 1/2" tall. **$200-$250**

Velmoss Scroll wall pocket with small chip to back corner, unmarked, 11 1/2" tall. **$200-$250**

Venetian Line

Originally made around the turn of the 20th century, these utilitarian cooking wares came in a buff color, pale yellow, or with a robin's egg blue glaze. They have an embossed saw-tooth pattern and are usually marked. Later examples may also be found.

Venetian ovenware bowl in blue glaze, came with wire handle and wooden grip, impressed mark "Venetian Fireproof," 10 3/4" by 5 1/8".   **$200-$250**

Miniature Venetian ovenware bowl with wire handle and wooden grip, possibly a salesman's sample, impressed mark "Venetian," 3 1/2" diameter by 1 5/8" without handle. No established value.

Venetian ovenware bowl, came with wire handle and wooden grip, impressed indistinct mark, 8 1/4" by 4 1/8".   **$80-$100**

Victorian Art Pottery

From the mid-1920s and with more than a little art nouveau influence, this line often bears a stylized band of birds and leaves with glazes in dull brown, tan, and black. A very few have bright vivid colors. Pieces are usually unmarked or have an "Rv" ink stamp or foil label.

Victorian Art Pottery bulbous vase, restoration to drill hole on bottom, foil label, 9 1/2" by 9 1/2". **$350-$400**

Brown Victorian Art Pottery bulbous vessel, small nick to base, unmarked, 4 1/4" by 6". **$200-$225**

Two Victorian Art Pottery pieces: yellow bulbous vessel with line to rim and small blue jardinière with various minor chips, unmarked, 5 1/4" by 7 1/4" and 4 1/4" by 6". **$300-$350/pair**

Two Victorian Art Pottery vessels in typical brown and tan colors: left, 258-7", unmarked, **$350-$400**; right, 132-4", with "Rv" ink stamp. **$300-$350**

Vista

The design of this line has prompted some to call it "Forest" because the lower half of the vessels look like tree trunks set in a watery landscape, but the top half of the vessels are clearly large-petal flowers that continue in an unbroken vista. Hues are a wet, watercolor green, lavender, and burgundy on a gray background. Pieces are usually unmarked or ink stamped in rare instances.

Vista vase, several lines from rim, a couple of small chips at base, unmarked, 14 1/2" by 4 1/4".
$650-$750

Vista bulbous vase, unmarked, 17 1/2" by 7 1/2".
$1,500-$1,700

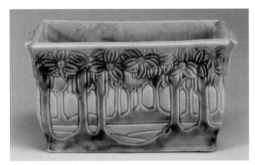

Vista basket, short line to handle, rare, 8 1/2" by 6". **$650-$750**

Vista rectangular planter, peppering to rim and some minor nicks, unmarked, rare, 6 1/4" by 11 1/2". **$1,300-$1,500**

Vista basket, unmarked, 6 3/4" by 4 3/4". **$450-$550**

Vista jardinière, small chip to rim, unmarked, 9 3/4" tall. **$325-$375**

Vista floor vase/umbrella stand, some minor flecks, unmarked, 20" by 9 1/2". **$1,600-$1,800**

Vista tapering vase, long tight line from rim, 15" by 6". **$900-$1,000**

Left: Vista low bowl, good color and mold, stamped 246, 3 1/4" by 7". **$175-$225**

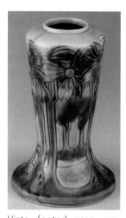

Vista footed vase, unmarked, 10" by 6 1/4". **$600-$700**

Vista wall pocket, some small chips and nicks, unmarked, 8 3/4". **$450-$550**

Vista jardinière and pedestal in as-is condition (chips, cracks, etc.), unmarked; pedestal: 18" tall, jardinière: 8 1/2" by 10". **$300-$350**

Vista hanging basket, firing lines to two handles, bruise to rim, and shallow spider line to base does not go through, unmarked, 3 1/2" by 6 3/4". **$200-$250**

Vista jardinière, some burst bubbles, unmarked, 6 1/2" by 7". **$275-$325** Left: Vista bowl, several chips to base, bruise and flecks to rim, unmarked, 6 3/4" diameter. **$150-$200**

Water Lily

The large flowers and lily pads on this line from 1943 float on a textured surface that resembles rippling water. Background colors are blue, brown, and pink, while the lily blossoms can be white, yellow, or lavender. Most pieces have raised marks.

Water Lily pink ewer (12-15"), repair to crack at spout and touch-up to one flower, raised mark.
$175-$225

Water Lily blue cookie jar (1-8"), raised mark, 9" by 10 1/4". **$400-$500**

Water Lily brown cookie jar (1-8"), strong mold, raised mark. **$400-$450**

Water Lily pink cookie jar (1-8"), pinhead-sized fleck to edge of rim and touch-up to nick and burst bubble on flower, raised mark. **$300-$400**

Water Lily pink bulbous vase (79-9"), small bruise to petal, raised mark.
$110-$140

Two Water Lily brown pieces: bulbous planter (663-5") with chip to one handle and corseted vase (80-10"), raised marks. **$110-$140/pair**

Three Water Lily pieces: blue vase (78-9"), brown jardinière (437-4"), and pink vase (71-4") with repair to rim, all marked. **$200-$250/set**

Left: Water Lily blue hanging basket, stamped "USA," 5 1/2" by 8 3/4".
$200-$225

White Rose

This line from 1940 features large blossoms on textured two-tone backgrounds of blue-turquoise, green-brown, and pink-green. Pieces feature raised marks.

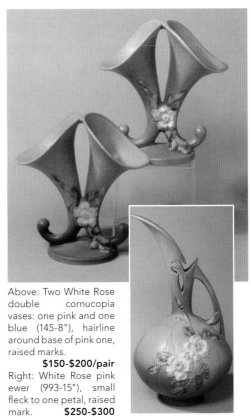

Above: Two White Rose double cornucopia vases: one pink and one blue (145-8"), hairline around base of pink one, raised marks.
$150-$200/pair

White Rose pink jardinière (656-10") and pedestal set, 1/4" chip to jardinière, both marked.
$700-$800

Right: White Rose pink ewer (993-15"), small fleck to one petal, raised mark. **$250-$300**

Pair of large White Rose blue bulbous vases (991-12"), nick and fleck to one, short tight line to rim of the other, raised marks. **$275-$325/pair**

Left: White Rose pink urn (991-12"), raised mark. **$175-$225**

Two White Rose blue pieces: flat vase (987-9") with dark crazing lines and fleck to one flower and bulbous vase (974-6"), raised marks.**$125-$175/pair**

White Rose blue tea set (1), raised marks; teapot: 7" by 8 1/4". **$300-$350/set**

Two White Rose wall pockets, one pink (1289-8") with minor firing flake near tip, and one brown (1288-6"), raised marks. **$450-$500/pair**

White Rose green basket (363-10"), raised mark. **$250-$300**

Two White Rose pieces: brown planter (387-4") with several chips to base and large blue bowl (394-14"), both marked.
$125-$175/pair

White Rose brown pitcher (990-10"), tight crack near spout, raised mark.
$90-$110

White Rose blue floor vase (994-16") with restoration to chips at rim, raised mark. **$250-$300**

White Rose brown pillow vase (984-8") with strong mold, raised mark.
$150-$200

White Rose brown bulbous vase (992-15"), good mold, raised mark.
$375-$425

Pair of White Rose vases, one blue and one pink (980-6"), raised marks.
$250-$300/pair

White Rose brown jardinière (653-6"), underglaze bruise to base, raised mark. **$110-$140**

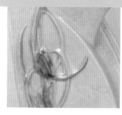

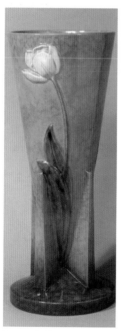

Wincraft

This line from 1948, with sleek designs and bright colors under a glossy finish, was named for then-company president Robert Windisch. There is really no consistent trait to these pieces other than the sheen. The company borrowed design elements from earlier lines and favored colors like chartreuse, apricot, and azure blue. Pieces usually have raised marks.

Wincraft floor vase with buttressed base (289-18") with ivory roses on a mottled vermillion ground, small 1/2" chip under the base, raised mark.
$400-$500

Trial matte glaze Wincraft flaring footed vase decorated with arrowroot plant on a shaded yellow and red ground (2V2-10"), raised mark with glaze codes, 10 1/4" by 5 1/2".
$750

Wincraft flaring vase (275-12") with thistle on yellow/amber mottled ground, raised mark.
$300-$400

Wincraft cylindrical panther vase (290-11"), 2" hairline from rim, small flat chip to bottom, raised mark.
$350-$400

Wincraft brown coffee set (250) decorated with berries, raised marks; coffee pot: 9 1/2" by 7 3/4".
$350-$450/set

Left: Wincraft yellow footed dish with leaves and berries (228-12"), raised mark, 15 1/2" by 5 1/4" by 4 7/8".
$120-$140

Wincraft brown tea set (271) with minor underglaze flake to base of creamer, raised marks; teapot: 7" by 9 1/2".
$175-$200/set

Wincraft brown four-sided vase (274-7") with panels of blowing wind, a couple of very minor nicks, raised mark.
$110-$140

Two Wincraft blue pieces: vase (284-10") and basket (208-8"), raised marks.
$225-$275/pair

Wincraft blue flaring vase (2V2-8") on squat base, with pinecone, raised mark. **$90-$110**

Left: Wincraft wall pocket with ivy on a blue ground (267-5"), raised mark.
$150-$200

Above: Two Wincraft blue pieces: tall vase (263-14") and basket (208-8"), both decorated with blossoms and leaves, raised marks.**$350-$450/pair**
Right: Wincraft blue coffee set (250) with minor fleck to spout of creamer, raised marks; coffee pot: 9 3/4" by 8". **$300-$350/set**

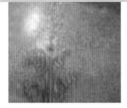

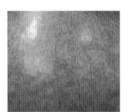

Windsor

Introduced in 1931, Windsor featured mottled glazes of muted blue and orange, decorated with floral motifs that were either stylized or impressionistic; some also have geometric patterns. Pieces are unmarked or have a foil label.

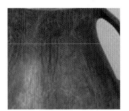

Windsor orange trumpet vase impressed with abstract pattern in green, unmarked, 7 1/4" by 4 1/2". **$450-$500**

Windsor gourd-shaped urn decorated with green fern, foil label, 9 1/4" by 6 1/4". **$1,300-$1,500**

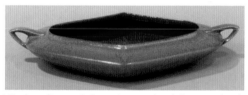

Windsor spherical lamp base impressed with green ferns on a mottled blue ground, drilled, 1" glaze scaling to handle, unmarked; pottery: 7" by 7 1/4". **$550-$650**

Windsor blue bulbous vessel impressed with geometric pattern around neck in yellow and green, unmarked, 6 1/4" by 6 1/4". **$400-$500**

Windsor blue bulbous urn impressed with stylized floral design in green and yellow, foil label, 5 1/4" by 4 3/4". **$375-$425**

Windsor diamond-shaped center bowl decorated with green oak leaves and acorns, minor burst bubble to tip of one handle, unmarked, 2 1/4" by 16". **$350-$400**

Windsor orange vase decorated with green geometric pattern around neck, black label, 6 1/4" by 6 1/4". **$375-$400**

Windsor orange diamond-shaped center bowl crisply decorated with green oak leaves and acorns, restoration to one handle, unmarked, 2 1/4" by 16". **$150-$200**

Right: Windsor orange squat low bowl with impressed decoration of stylized green leaves and peas, flower frog, 1/2" chip to base of flower frog, foil label to one; bowl: 2 3/4" by 12".
$200-$250

Wisteria

Wisteria from 1937 features large pink or lavender hanging blooms and leaves on a textured surface. Though collectors typically refer to blue or brown pieces, both colors can be found on the same piece, with one dominating, accented by yellow or green. Pieces are unmarked or have foil labels.

Wisteria brown jardinière and pedestal, several tight cracks through base and minor bruise to one flower of jardinière; pedestal mint, unmarked; jardinière: 10" tall; pedestal: 18" tall. **$1,700-$1,900**

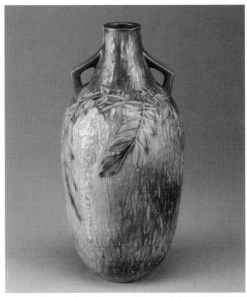

Wisteria brown bottle-shaped vase, foil label, 15 1/4" tall. **$1,600-$1,800**

Wisteria blue bottle-shaped vase with excellent mold and color, bruise to rim, unmarked, 15" by 7 1/2".
$2,100-$2,300

Wisteria blue gourd-shaped vase, foil label, 7 1/2" by 5 1/2".
$900-$1,000

Wisteria blue bulbous vase, minute fleck to rim, gold foil label, 8 1/4" by 6 1/4". **$1,100-$1,300**

Wisteria blue flaring vase with strong mold, unmarked, 8 1/4".
$700-$800

Left: Wisteria blue hanging basket with strong mold, some nicks and flecks, two opposing hairlines, chip to both handles, unmarked, 4 1/2" by 7 1/2". **$400-$500**

Wisteria blue cylindrical two-handled vase, strong mold and color, minor nick to petal, unmarked, 10 1/4" by 6 1/4".
$900-$1,200

Wisteria blue wall pocket with strong mold and color, unmarked, 8 1/2" by 7". **$1,650-$1,750**

Wisteria blue squat vessel with closed in rim, foil label, 5 1/4" by 6 1/2".
$400-$500

Wisteria brown tapering vase, unmarked, 10 1/2" tall. **$900-$1,000**

Wisteria brown two-handled classically shaped vessel with strong mold and color, two small glaze flakes at base, unmarked, 8 1/4" by 7 1/2".
$400-$450

Wisteria brown bulbous vase, nick to body and minor bruise to one flower, unmarked, 6 3/4" by 8".
$450-$550

Wisteria brown gourd-shaped vase, crisp mold and good color, unmarked, 8 1/4" by 4 1/2".
$450-$550

Wisteria brown corseted two-handled vase with strong mold and color, 1/2" chip with bruise to one handle, gold foil label, 10 1/2" by 8".
$450-$500

Wisteria brown squat vessel with good mold and color, gold foil label, 4 1/2" by 5 3/4". **$300-$400**

Wisteria brown gourd-shaped vase, foil label, 7" by 6". **$400-$450**

Wisteria brown four-sided planter with good mold, unmarked, 3 1/4" by 12". **$350-$400**

Zephyr Lily

This line from 1946 features blossoms of white, yellow, rose, and lavender (often two bloom colors on the same piece) on a textured background that looks like a pool rippling with raindrops. Body colors are variegated blues, browns, and greens. Pieces have raised marks.

Far left: Zephyr Lily brown jardinière (671-8"), firing bruise to base and a few small flecks to high points, raised mark. **$225-$275** Left: Zephyr Lily blue hanging basket, marked "U.S.A.," 6" by 7 1/2".
$125-$175

Zephyr Lily green jardinière (671-8") and pedestal, a few minor flecks to rim and body, raised mark to jardinière and "U.S.A." mark to pedestal.
$450-$500

Zephyr Lily blue floor vase (142-18"), restoration to small chips on handles, raised mark. **$450-$500**

Zephyr Lily blue wall pocket (1297-8"), small flakes to base. **$150-$200**

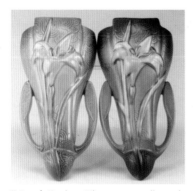

Pair of Zephyr Lily green wall pockets (1297-8"), nick to tip of one, both marked. **$200-$250/pair**

Two green Zephyr Lily vases, 136-9" with repair to rim chip, and 140-12", both marked. **$250-$300/pair**

Zephyr Lily brown tea set (7) with small burst bubble to creamer, raised marks; teapot: 7" by 9 1/4". **$350-$450/set**

Zephyr Lily brown cookie jar (5-8"), chip to one flower and small chips to lid rim, raised mark. **$300-$350**

Two Zephyr Lily pieces: blue vase (137-10") with flaring rim (1/4" chip at rim) and brown pillow vase (205-6") with a couple of shallow scratches to base, raised marks. **$110-$140/pair**

Three Zephyr Lily pieces: blue flaring vase (136-9") with nick to base and pair of brown bookends (16), all marked; bookends: 5 1/4" tall each. **$225-$275/pair**

Reproductions

Roseville Pottery has been reproduced in china since 1996. The majority of reproductions have a fake version of Roseville's Late Period mark, the word Roseville in script above a shape/size number. Original marks include U.S.A. between Roseville" and the shape/size number. The comparable fake mark does not include U.S.A.

On some of the earliest reproductions you may find U.S.A. in very faint weak letters like the examples shown here. In original Late Period marks used 1935-1954, the U.S.A. is the same height and sharpness as Roseville and the shape/size number. The only exceptions are particularly small original shapes where there was no space for U.S.A.

Reproductions of Roseville's pre-1934 patterns have begun appearing with the mark shown here. Although this is a close copy of an authentic pre-1934 Roseville mark, it is easily detected. The original mark is impressed below the surface; the fake mark is molded and raised above the surface.

A typical authentic Roseville mark used during the Late Period, 1935-1954. Note that U.S.A. is the same height and weight as Roseville and the shape/size number. If U.S.A. is missing or very faint in the Late Period mark, it is almost certainly a reproduction.

A typical fake mark found on the majority of Roseville reproductions made in China. This example is shown with the removable paper label as it arrives from the reproduction wholesaler. In fake marks, the letters U.S.A. are either missing or, as in this example, very faint.

A fake raised mark used on reproductions of Roseville Middle Period patterns such as Jonquil and Luffa. Original Luffa and Jonquil never had raised marks. Original Luffa and Jonquil usually had paper labels only, never raised molded marks.

Bottom Marks

There is no consistency to Roseville bottom marks. Even within a single popular pattern like Pine Cone, the marks vary.

Several shape numbering systems were implemented during the company's 64-year history, with some denoting a vessel style and some applied to separate lines. Though many pieces are unmarked, from 1900 until the late teens or early 1920s, Roseville used a variety of marks including "RPCo," "Roseville Pottery Company," and the word "Rozane," the last often with a line name, i.e., "Egypto."

The underglaze ink script "Rv" mark was used on lines introduced from the mid-to-late teens through the mid-1920s. Around 1926 or 1927, Roseville began to use a small, triangular black paper label on lines such as Futura and Imperial II. Silver or gold foil labels began to appear around 1930, continuing for several years on lines such as Blackberry and Tourmaline, and on some early Pine Cone.

From 1932 to 1937, an impressed script mark was added to the molds used on new lines, and around 1937 the raised script mark was added to the molds of new lines. The relief mark includes "U.S.A."

All bottom mark images appear courtesy Adamstown Antique Gallery, Adamstown, Pennsylvania.

Impressed numeral on Crocus urn, 6" tall.

Unmarked base and side-marked initials (possibly Harry Larzelere) on Della Robbia vase, 7" tall.

Wafer mark and incised artist's initials on Della Robbia vase, 10" tall.

Wafer mark on Della Robbia vase, 10 1/2" tall.

Wafer on Egypto ewer, 11" tall.

Wafer on Egypto vase, 9" tall.

Grease pencil marks on Falline spherical vase, 6" tall.

Ink stamp on Falline bulbous vase, 7" tall.

Unmarked base of Ferella vase, 6" tall.

Ink stamp on Florentine I 10" jardinière.

Black paper label on Futura footed vessel, 4 1/2" tall.

Obscured ink stamp on Hexagon vase, 5" tall.

Marks on Imperial II squat vessel.

Gold foil label and grease pencil marks on Imperial II vase, 10" tall.

Impressed mark on Iris vase.

Raised mark on Lotus vase in a trial glaze, 10" tall.

Faint impressed mark on Mara vase, 8" tall.

Obscured marks on Morning Glory vase, 10" tall.

Ink stamp on Panel vase with nudes, 10" tall.

Impressed mark on Pine Cone blue cider pitcher.

Ink stamps and gold foil label on Pine Cone blue spherical planter.

Raised mark on Pine Cone blue pillow vase.

Impressed and incised marks on Pine Cone blue vase.

Faint impressed and ink stamps on Pine Cone blue vase.

Impressed mark on Pine Cone green footed planter.

Impressed marks on Rozane portrait vase, 13" tall.

Marks on Russco bulbous urn, 6 1/2" tall.

Raised mark and ink stamp on Silhouette brown vase.

Raised mark and ink stamp on Silhouette red vase.

Faint mark on Sunflower bulbous vessel, 4" tall.

Faint ink stamp and grease pencil on Velmoss pink vase.

Raised mark on Water Lily brown floor vase.

Raised mark on Wincraft cylindrical panther vase, 11" tall.

Incised mark on Windsor bulbous vessel.

Ink stamps on Wisteria bowl, 5" tall.

Faint ink stamp on Wisteria bulbous vase, 8" tall.

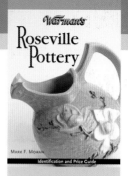

Travel the
world
of
Roseville
with an
expert!

krause publications
An Imprint of F+W Publications

700 East State Street • Iola, WI 54990-0001
715-445-2214 • 888-457-2873

To order call
800-258-0929

M-F 7 am - 8 pm
Sat. 8 am - 2 pm, CST

Offer ACB6

Shipping & Handling: $4 for first book, $2.25 each additional. Non-US addresses $20.95 first book, $5.95 each additional.
Sales Tax: CA, IA, IL, KS, NJ, PA, SD, TN, VA, WI residents add appropriate sales tax.

Warman's® Roseville Pottery
Identification and Price Guide
by Mark F. Moran
Softcover • 8¼ x 10⅞
• 256 pages • 1,200 color photos
Item# RVPT • $24.99

Peer over the shoulder of renown antiques dealer and author, Mark F. Moran in this exciting book, to learn more about the wonderful world of Roseville! Captivating history, thorough condition reports, real-world prices, and reproduction alerts make this complete reference more than your basic price guide.

The information in this beautifully illustrated book will give you the details, historical background and pricing insight to make smart purchases, and accurately assess the worth of your collection. In the pages of this must-have resource, you'll find:

> Detailed descriptions of the pieces listed - right down to the length of hairlines and the position of "flea-bite" nicks - to help make identification easy

> More than 1,200 color photographs which showcase the beauty and brilliance of Roseville pottery, and assist with accurately identifying pieces

> Expertly researched real-world prices that reflect the true value of pottery, based on decades of use and storage

> Historical information to help new collectors gain knowledge to enhance their collection

This book is a wonderful reference for the beginning collector, and a great guide for experienced collectors looking for a quick overview of Roseville.